Cambridge Wizard Student Guide

Oedipus Rex

Kilian McNamara

B.A., Dip.Ed., Grad.Dip.Curriculum

CAMBRIDGE
UNIVERSITY PRESS

CAMBRIDGE UNIVERSITY PRESS
Cambridge, New York, Melbourne, Madrid, Cape Town, Singapore, São Paulo

Cambridge University Press
477 Williamstown Road, Port Melbourne, VIC 3207, Australia

www.cambridge.edu.au

First published in 2003
Reprinted 2005

Cover design by Cressaid Media
Cover art by Valerie Den Ouden
Text design by Sarn Potter
Typeset by Kelsey Burge

Printed in Australia by Print Impressions

Typeface Berkeley *System* PageMaker® [KB]

National Library of Australia Cataloguing in Publication data
    McNamara, Killian, 1952–.
    Oedipus Rex
    ISBN 0 521 53616 2.
    1. Sophocles. Oedipus Rex. I. Title. (Series: Cambridge wizard students guide).
822.01

ISBN 0 521 53616 2 paperback

Contents

Notes on the Author   5

Notes on Greek Tragedy   7

Notes on Genre, Structure and Style   10

Summary and Commentary   14

Notes on Characters   40

Notes on Themes and Issues   46

What the Critics Say   58

Writing an Essay on the Text   59

Sample Essay   61

Essay Questions   63

Notes on the Author

Sophocles (pronounced Sof-o-kleez) was one of the greatest writers of antiquity. He is generally considered the pre-eminent tragedian of classical Greece, and therefore a key figure in world literature. Although plays like *Oedipus Rex* are 2500 years old, among the oldest works in history attributable to a specific author, they are still performed. Sophocles helped mould the whole tradition of tragedy (a major literary genre), and his influence is felt to this day.

Sophocles was born at Colonus, near Athens, in 496 BC. Raised within a wealthy family, he enjoyed the benefits of a good education which enabled him to flourish from an early age as a noted dancer, musician and playwright. He was considered an important citizen of Athens, and was several times elected to high office.

It is as a writer however that we best know him. He inherited from earlier tragedians such as Aeschylus (see following notes on Greek Tragedy) the basic form of Greek theatre, which consisted of a 'cast' of two actors (swapping roles between scenes) and a 'chorus'. He was to add a third actor, thereby greatly increasing the dramatic potential of the form. Out of these simple materials, using traditional stories, brought to life in brilliant verse, he composed an estimated 120 plays. In 468BC, when he was still only 28, he beat the famous Aeschylus at the annual Athenian drama contest. This win established Sophocles at the forefront of Greek drama, a position he was never to forfeit. In all, he probably won first prize on at least eighteen occasions. *Oedipus Rex* (also known as *King Oedipus*, and *Oedipus Tyrannos*), written in 429BC, is his best known work. It forms part of a trilogy now known collectively as 'The Theban Plays' (since they concern the royal family of Thebes, a major Greek city), though they were written years apart and in a different order to the anthologised one. The other two plays in the trilogy are *Oedipus at Colonus* (401BC) and *Antigone* (441BC).

In his earlier years Sophocles was known for his love of the sensuous delights and this reputation was never to desert him. Yet, for all his enjoyment of the good life, his plays are deeply rooted in the religious traditions from which Greek drama sprang. *Oedipus Rex* reflects this underlying conservatism. It could be said that

Sophocles worked from the 'inside' of the political establishment all his life. A close political ally of the great Athenian leader, Pericles, he sought to develop in dramatic terms many of the qualities of the ideal Athenian, considered the perfect expression of civilised 'man'. During Sophocles' life, Athens reached the height of its power, both politically and culturally. It effectively ruled Greece, and the city was the centre of a brilliant culture that gave us not only theatre, but also philosophy, science, mathematics, democracy, poetry, medicine and some of the greatest art of all time.

Only towards the end of his long life did the political intrigues and conflicts of that era impinge upon him personally. Athens was by then embroiled in wars with its neighbouring states (particularly the warrior state Sparta) and the older Sophocles became a general, even if only in name. Perhaps fortunately for him, he was to die before the final humiliation of Athens – its defeat by Sparta in 404BC – closed off the great era of artistic and cultural achievement we now know as the 'golden age' of ancient Greece.

Notes on Greek Tragedy

If there is much about the theatrical traditions of ancient Greece which seem alien to us, we should, nonetheless make some effort to grasp their broad outlines. Certainly one cannot approach any study of *Oedipus Rex* without this background knowledge.

The point of theatre to the ancient Greeks

The experience of going to the 'theatre' in ancient Greece was markedly different from anything one would expect today. It was, first and foremost, part of a religious pageant or festival. Theatrical events, in honour of the god, Dionysius, would take place over several days, usually during the season of Spring. Dionysius was the god of revelry, and the cultic groups associated with him revelled in drunken excess and sexual licence!

In addition, 'going to the theatre' was in many ways an act of citizenship. It was a public declaration of a civilised interest in the arts, in religious observance. It offered a chance for the Athenian citizen to ponder the issues of public morality, of human vanity and our relationships with the capricious gods. In plays, one saw the mighty humbled and the heroic virtues extolled. It is difficult to think of a modern ceremony which offers equivalent possibilities for the parade of civic virtue.

What were classical plays like?

Strict conventions surrounded the performance of these plays. They may seem odd to us, but there were strong historical reasons for the conventions.

The origins of Greek theatre

Theatre had evolved over centuries out of the rituals of the Dionysian festival. In very early times, there were no actors – just a 'chorus' (or choir). It is believed that around 501BC, a performer called Thespis introduced the idea of someone playing a part. This novelty allowed a primitive form of 'dialogue' to take place between the 'thespian' (actor) and the chorus. During the golden age of classical drama, Aeschylus introduced a second actor, allowing genuine, flexible interchanges. It is said that Sophocles

Theatre in the time of Sophocles

himself introduced a third actor. Because of the stylised, ritual aspects of the performance (akin to a religious ceremony, but with a story), everything was said in a very formal, 'declamatory' style.

By the time of Sophocles, three actors were allowed on stage at the same time. They were ranked: the protagonist (number one actor), who in the case of *Oedipus Rex* would be the actor playing Oedipus himself; the deuteragonist (number two), who might play several roles; and the tritagonist (number three) who would also pick up several roles. In between scenes, the actors retired and either waited for their next appearance (in the case of the protagonist) or swapped masks and costumes to take up another role (in the case of the lower ranked actors). This system allowed the playwright to create a 'script' using up to about eight characters (because the actors swapped roles several times). They were all men. Women were not allowed to participate. The Chorus, a group of singer-dancers, chanted in unison, commenting on the action as it unfolded.

The costumes

All actors wore masks, customised to show the sort of character (man, woman, king, prophet) they were impersonating, and often they would wear specific dresses and colours to denote their social status. Different masks were worn to distinguish comedy (a laughing or grotesquely caricatured mask) from tragedy (a suffering mask). Many of the costumes and headdresses worn were larger than life, and often they wore padding. The actors typically wore high boots (up to 300mm) to make them easier to see, as well as to emphasise the status of the wearer.

The structure of Greek tragedy

Each tragedy was constructed on strict, traditional lines. They were as follows:

- **Prologos** (prologue) – in which the background and overall lines of the story were sketched, to enhance audience understanding
- **Parados** – the ritual entrance of the Chorus, and their opening speech
- **Episode One** – in effect what we would call an 'act', with multiple 'scenes'
- **Stasimon One** – a choric ode, in which the chorus commented on what had just happened (this was to draw out the 'moral' of the action, to highlight themes or to anticipate issues which might arise)
- **Episode Two**, followed by Stasimon Two
- **Episode Three**, followed by Stasimon Three
- **Episode Four**, followed by Stasimon Four
- **Episode Five**, followed by
- **Exodos** (the final speech of the Chorus), or epilogue, in which all the key issues/themes of the play were summed up and the aftermath indicated.

Oedipus Rex follows this structure very closely. If we think about it, a Shakespearean play has a very similar structure – five acts – with the prologue integrated into Act One and the epilogue into Act Five.

What was the theatre like?

The performance space

The theatre itself was an open air ampitheatre with none of the fixed individual seating of the modern theatre, nor what we regard as the 'traditional' proscenium arch.

In front of the stage was a raised section known as the *parados*, upon which the chorus would stand. Chanting and dancing, as well as reciting long set speeches, songs and poems, they provided a link between the action happening on stage and the audience. In the case of *Oedipus Rex*, they often play the role of a detached commentator, enhancing our understanding of the story in terms of its political and religious significance.

Performance

The actors performed on a circular flat area directly in front of the audience called the *orchestra*. Behind them was a low building with doors for entrances and exits, and revealed tableaux, called the *skene*. Above the skene there would often appear the *mechane* (or *machina*), a large crane-like device which allowed various characters to be 'flown' in from above. Often they would be godlike creatures, capable of superhuman feats.

The performances always took place during daylight. Greek theatres were vast, accomodating up to 10,000 people at a time. Their size, and grandeur testify to the cultural importance and popularity of drama.

Notes on Genre, Structure and Style

Genre

Oedipus Rex is quite simply the most famous of all Greek tragedies. In *The Poetics* – perhaps the earliest example of what we would now call literary theory – Aristotle (384-322BC) described it as a masterpiece, and used it as an example of perfect form.

Tragedy

So what was tragedy? It is arguably the greatest part of what we now call Greek theatre (the other two forms being comedy and the satyr plays). It must be understood on its own terms. For what the audiences of that time took from the word *tragedy* is quite different from our modern conceptions.

Greek tragedy arose from a long tradition of choral singing. In extended verse form, stories from the past – the myths and legends of the Greek gods and heroes – came to be handed down from generation to generation. Generally those tales were of great men and women, creatures who seemed larger than life. The stories told of their great feats and their valour. More importantly, they told of the relationships between these legendary folk and the gods. By extension, they offered a profound commentary on morality and life itself.

The concept of the tragic flaw

A Greek tragedy involved great men and women struggling with the often malevolent forces of fate. Inevitably, there was a disastrous outcome. Typically, the great man would be toppled because of some fatal flaw (the Greek word is *hamartia*), a kind of moral blindness, which was seen as the cause of the downfall appear inevitable.

Grasping this concept is central to understanding tragedy. Aristotle was later to define a classical tragedy this way:

> **Quote**
>
> The [tragedy] must not be a spectacle of a virtuous man brought from prosperity to adversity: for this moves neither pity nor fear; it merely shocks us; nor again, that of a bad man passing from adversity to prosperity...[It must concern] a man who is not eminently good and just, yet whose misfortune is brought about not by vice or depravity, but by some error or frailty. (*The Poetics*)

If we put this into modern language, we could say: the tragic hero (or heroine) is not a perfect man, but he is certainly *not* a bad man; the key to what happens is that he is undone by one fatal weakness – usually *hubris* (pride) – which cancels out his good intentions, and brings him down. Too much bad, and we are not displeased that he is ruined. We possibly even celebrate his downfall. Too much good, and we are offended (because it seems unfair). The balance is a delicate one, but the connection between a fault (*hamartia*) and tragedy is a crucial part of the theory – and it rules much of literature to this day.

The concept of 'hubris' (pride)

In the case of *Oedipus Rex*, Oedipus seems indeed to be a victim of *hamartia* – and his particular fault is *hubris*. He is a man of great achievements, yet he is arrogant – and his arrogance has led to the 'sins' he commits – the killing of Laius and the marrying of Jocasta. Furthermore, even his discovery of the crimes is partly attributable to his headstrong qualities. He cannot see what is apparent to others, that his quest to uncover the truth of his origins can only be a path to madness. For this fault he will pay dearly.

Greek tragedy is essentially about the mixed and tortuous nature of human psychology, its breathtaking capacity for paradox: the heights of altruism and nobility, the depths of selfishness and evil. In a tragedy, we see these eternal psychic (and moral) forces in collision, spelt out in the dread tale of one such wretch, and we are meant to learn from it.

Structure

Structurally, as already noted, Oedipus Rex is the classic Greek tragedy. It has the following:

- Prologos (the prologue) – the problem is announced: a pestilence grips Thebes, and it is discovered that the cause is a divine curse because the killer of the old king Laius has not been brought to justice
- Parados – the Chorus call on the gods for help
- Episode One – Oedipus pronounces a curse on the murderer and begins the investigation; Teiresias (the seer) is provoked into telling Oedipus that *he* is the guilty person
- Stasimon One – the Chorus comments on the investigation
- Episode Two – Oedipus accuses Creon of putting Teiresias up to the accusation; Jocasta tries to calm him, telling him of the 'false' prophecy about her child;

Oedipus in turn tells her the story of his attempts to escape the curse of his birth

- Stasimon Two – the Chorus warn of the dangers of pride
- Episode Three – a Messenger brings news that King Polybus of Corinth has died, thereby disproving the curse; he goes on to say, however, that Oedipus was *not* the son of Polybus (as he imagined); Jocasta, grasping the truth, tries to stop Oedipus investigating, but in vain
- Stasimon Three – the Chorus comment that the truth will soon be known
- Episode Four – the old Shepherd who is a key witness confesses, against his will, that Oedipus is the child of Laius and Jocasta; Oedipus is devastated
- Stasimon Four – the Chorus laments the illusion of happiness, and the fall of Oedipus
- Episode Five – a royal Attendant describes the suicide of Jocasta, and how Oedipus, finding her body, has blinded himself; Oedipus shows himself; Creon (the new king) lets him say goodbye to his daughters, before sending him into exile
- Exodos (the final speech of the Chorus), or epilogue – the Chorus bemoans the tragedy of Oedipus, and its implications for all mankind.

The play as a murder mystery

From a narrative point of view, the play follows a traditional 'mystery' form – with the exposition (Prologue) announcing the crime (and the desperate need for it to be solved), and the first four 'Acts' devoted to the investigation. The ghastly irony in this play is that the culprit turns out to be none other than the investigator, a brilliant piece of plot symmetry, as well as a breathtaking thematic comment (on Oedipus' 'blindness' about his faults). The mystery is solved by the end of Episode 4, leaving only the full enactment of the tragedy proper – Episode 5, in which the fatal aftermath is detailed – the suicide, the self-mutilation, the exile.

The classical 'unities'

Sophocles was an acknowledged master of the form, and *Oedipus Rex* is considered his masterpiece. Nowhere is his skill more obvious perhaps than in the perfect structure of the work. From the opening Prologos in which Oedipus innocently asks what is wrong, to the lamentation of the Exodos, just after he is led away for good, the action rolls forward with awesome power. There are no quiet spots, no digressions, no irrelevancies. Not a line is wasted. The whole story takes place in a single place (the palace of Thebes) in a single day, and concerns a single theme (the pride and fall of one man). It thus obeys what are called the classical 'unities' (time, place, theme) – considered essential in the creation of great tragedy.

Style

Stylistically, the play resembles other Greek tragedies, insofar as it uses grand and poetic language (the original is in verse), suitable to the vast themes of the work. We must be a little cautious in talking of the language, for we are reading it in an English translation. However, it is clear that this is the product of a brilliant writer.

Although the characters 'declaim' in a theatrical fashion – not in the idiom of modern realist theatre or television – that (formal eloquence) is exactly what the ancient audience would have expected. If we think of the language of a church service (say a funeral mass), or the Bible, we are getting close to the sort of linguistic weight with which this text tells its tragic story. The characters speak the 'high' language of myths and religion. The ancient Greeks had their vernacular (street talk), like anyone, but a tragedy was not the place for it.

Characterisation there is, certainly. Oedipus gets angry, and threatens, and (later) pleads. Jocasta's horror is well expressed. But always the words are delivered with the 'monumental' language considered appropriate to so serious a literary form. If we could read the original Greek, and see the sheer beauty of the verse, we would experience something like the thrill readers know in reading one of the immortal passages from Shakespeare. Even in translation, this grandeur is not entirely lost, and we should bear it in mind when responding to the text.

NB To make the plot summary in this guide easier to follow, we have divided the play into its main structural components – including the Parados, the Episodes, the Stasimons (choric odes) and the Exodos. Within the episodes we have broken the action down into various 'scenes' – each with a title to aid identification. In the original play, however, the action is continuous, and such discrete 'scenes' do not exist. All quotations made in this study guide come from the translation by E.F. Watling (Penguin, 1947)

Summary and Commentary

Prologos (Prologue)

The problem

Before the Royal Palace of Thebes, a group of concerned citizens have assembled. The king, Oedipus, appears, and asks them what troubles them. The leader, a priest, beseeches the king's help. The Priest tells him of the **city's 'affliction'**, how death is all around them, in the 'fruitful flowering' of the soil, in the pastures, and 'in the womb of woman'. It is, indeed, a **'fiery demon' which is 'gripping the city'**. He recalls that it was Oedipus who came to the town and broke their bondage to the Sphinx, that 'vile Enchantress'. Now, it is to Oedipus, the man who has delivered them from past strife that his plea is directly made. Can he help them once again?

Oedipus asserts that he too suffers. The collective grief of his people weigh heavily upon him. However, he has already taken action – sending his kinsman Creon to the temple of Apollo (the god of healing) for divine advice – to learn what Oedipus might do to ease the situation.

Advice from the god

At this moment, Creon is seen in the distance. It seems that he brings glad tidings. His head is crowned with bay leaves. Oedipus entreats him to speak to the assembled multitude. If this is good news, it must be shared.

The curse is revealed

Creon's report from Phoebus (Apollo) is that there is an **'unclean thing' defiling their city** and that this is the source of their troubles. This person was 'born and nursed' in their fair city and is now 'polluting' its soil. He must be 'driven away'. The only expiation acceptable to the gods is the banishment of such a man, or **'the payment of blood for blood'**. For it was the original shedding of the blood of King Laius which has led to these calamities. The 'unknown killer' must now be brought to justice.

Oedipus enquires further about the crime and is told by Creon that the murder took place outside their country. Only one man survived as a witness to the terrible events and he flew in terror. No proper investigation could be launched, as the Sphinx had diverted the citizens' attention to more pressing matters.

Oedipus
commits to
finding the
killer

Oedipus promises to devote all his energies to unmasking the killer of Laius. Indeed, the killer might one day threaten him! In closing, the priest dismisses the suppliants. He prays that Phoebus (Apollo), from whom this answer came, may yet **'deliver'** them of their **'heavy afflictions'**.

Parados (entrance and introductory speech of the Chorus)

The Chorus of Theban elders now speaks of the great fear which has gripped the fair city of Thebes. Calling upon the gods for help, they tell of the **'sickness'** which is rife among them; from **'fire and pain of pestilence'** they beg to be delivered. **The city now 'reeks' with 'death in all her streets'**, while mothers 'at every altar kneel', calling upon (the goddess) Athena for help. It is a **'Death God'** which must be slain, not with 'the rattle of bronze', but with a fiery torch which only the gods can wield.

Commentary
First task: the
narrative
exposition

The first task of a writer in any medium is to set the scene. This 'exposition' function is the prime reason for the Prologue. Notice how skilfully Sophocles accomplishes his exposition – contextualising and informing while also initiating the drama.

The king's opening speech does not start with florid assertions, or descriptions, but with a question: 'What is the meaning of this supplication (desperate plea)?' That leads us straight to the problem which has to be resolved by the narrative:

Beginning
of action

the terrible pestilence that has overtaken Thebes. And so the 'action' of the play gets under way, immediately. The mystery of the city's strange 'affliction' is set before us, a mystery which will drive all the actions of Oedipus and those he enlists in his fatal search for the truth. By the time Creon has delivered his news – that the murder of the old king Laius is the reason for the 'curse' – we have all the background we need for the whole tale. The Prologue has done its work: now it is time for the 'investigation', the main story.

Introduction
to the
protagonist

We know what is driving the narrative straight away (the pestilence – the curse behind it – the murder which brought on the curse – the 'investigation' which will solve the murder). What about those involved? Here the playwright's subtlety is worth noting. For we learn a lot about Oedipus, even before the story proper has started. What do we learn?

Oedipus the hero

Oedipus comes across as a good king. He 'willingly' listens to the citizens. He grieves for them. He weeps. Their plight concerns him, he says, 'more than my life'. When the curse is revealed, he loses no time in opening the investigation: he will find out who killed Laius. Here is Oedipus the problem-solver, the man of action, the natural leader. He appears just, merciful, politic, even kind. These are royal qualities and not to be lightly dismissed. In many ways he fits the definition of the ideal Athenian outlined by the great ruler, Pericles. The audience witnessing Sophocles' play would have been well aware of these ideal qualities, and how much they were embodied in the noble figure of Oedipus.

And all these qualities are important. Oedipus is a great man – 'the first of men', the Chorus calls him. He is well-intentioned. That we perceive him thus is vital – as explained in the introductory notes – for the whole point of tragedy is how faults can undo even good intentions, and bring a person down.

Oedipus the proud man

Is anything else revealed? Indeed. Beneath these good qualities are hints of something else. **'I, Oedipus, whose name is known afar,'** he says, in his first speech. Arguably, there is an element of self-dramatisation in **'none suffers more than I'**. **'I have not been idle,'** he boasts, and **'I…will bring everything into the light'**. Most interesting perhaps, is his immediately sensing that whoever killed Laius may go on 'to turn his hand against me'. Along with his good qualities, self-glorification, and a hint of narcissism, is emerging.

Dramatic irony (the audience knows something the characters do not know)

And let us not forget the terrible irony in all this. Greek tragedy is predicated upon the notion that a great and wise leader (such as Oedipus) suffers from the fatal flaw of pride – *hubris* – which will surely be their eventual undoing. Oedipus' pronouncements are heavily laden with dramatic irony. For he is talking with horror about uncovering the killer of Laius, and as we (and the ancient audience) know already, that is Oedipus himself. *We* know what *he* as yet doesn't! Worse still are these lines:

> Quote

The killer of Laius
Whoever he was, might think to turn his hand
Against me…

and

Quote

> Certain it is
> That by the help of God we stand – or fall.

Both of these will turn out to be predictions: the killer of Laius (Oedipus) will turn his hand against the king (also, by an excruciating irony Oedipus), and by the will of the gods Oedipus will 'fall'.

The role of the Chorus

While Oedipus dominates the play already, the role of the Chorus is also of great interest. To modern ears, their pious prayers to the gods may seem at best mere decoration or ritual, at worst an irrelevant interruption to the action. But we must not dismiss them too quickly. While Oedipus is a character in his own right, a great but wilful and fatal figure, the Chorus symbolise something more mundane – the 'common man'. They just want to have peace and harmony. For them, glory and self-assertion are not an issue – they simply want to end the pestilence and live in security again. To whom do they turn? To the *gods* themselves. They implore Apollo (Healer of Delos, and 'Phoebus'), Athena, Zeus, Artemis and Bacchus to come to their aid. Oedipus may have been arrogantly assuring the citizens that they should leave all these matters in his hands, but the Chorus want to show their piety and bow down to the might of forces greater than man.

The argument

They are in effect ritually demonstrating the sort of humility which is diametrically opposed to the arrogance – *hubris* – of Oedipus. Thus the polarity between Oedipus and the Chorus in itself begins to look like an argument – *self* and *pride* (Oedipus), against *community* and *humility* (the Chorus). A sort of cosmic tension is being played out here, and it will be very significant within the play's subtext.

Episode (Act) 1

Scene 1 Oedipus addresses the Theban elders

Oedipus investigates

Oedipus speaks directly to the Theban elders, once more pledging himself to uncovering the agent of this crime against Laius.

If any of them have any knowledge about the foul deed, they should speak now. Silence greets these words. Oedipus goes on to offer clemency to any among them who may be harbouring guilty knowledge. Nothing worse than banishment will befall them. If they know of an alien who may have been the assassin, a large reward will be offered. Again, silence greets his every utterance. Finally Oedipus warns that if any of them is found to be shielding himself or another guilty party from scrutiny, a heavy sentence lies on his head. That man or men will be excommunicated from every house in his kingdom, forbidden to join in any prayer or sacrifice.

Oedipus and the 'self curse'

Nor does he spare himself or his house such heavy penalties. **'All the curses' on the guilty party will be laid upon him** if, with his knowledge, his 'house or hearth' ever made welcome the same man (the killer). Now that he is in control, he will fight for the cause of dead Laius as he would for his own father. He calls upon the gods to **'curse'** anyone who seeks to undermine his cause. He prays that **'Justice and all the gods'** be with them forever.

In reply, the Chorus pleads ignorance. The identity of the guilty man is a mystery to them. Surely, if the problem has been posed by Phoebus (Apollo), then *he* is the one to supply the answer. The Chorus offers hope in the form of Teiresias (a priest of Apollo). As one skilled in the arts of divination, he can perhaps help them in their quest. Oedipus agrees, telling the Chorus that the seer is on his way.

Scene 2 Teiresias and Oedipus

The blind seer Teiresias enters. Oedipus flatters him, saying that nothing is beyond his 'ken' (knowledge, or understanding). They look to him as 'their only help and protector'. He repeats Phoebus' conditions: the only way the city can be delivered from the plague is by finding out and killing or banishing the killer or killers of Laius.

Teiresias refuses to speak

Teiresias answers that **to be 'wise is to suffer'**. To spare both Oedipus and himself, he would rather be silent. Oedipus however is enraged at this apparent insolence and orders him to speak. Again Teiresias refuses, arguing that Oedipus should put his own house 'in order'.

The insults fly thick and fast until Teiresias can be silent no longer. In the face of Oedipus' accusation that it was he – Teiresias – who had some hand in the death of Laius, he launches a spirited attack upon Oedipus. Not he, but **Oedipus, is 'the cursed polluter of this land'**. The killer that Oedipus seeks is himself. Moreover Oedipus is now living in 'sinful union' with the woman he loves (Jocasta).

Oedipus is enraged. Branding **Teiresias a 'brainless,**

sightless, senseless sot' (drunkard) he taunts him for his blindness. Teiresias, he asserts, cannot hurt Oedipus, nor any man that 'sees the light'.

Oedipus suspects that the envious Creon lies behind these allegations. Teiresias assures him that it is not Creon who is the enemy, but himself. Oedipus blunders on. Where was Teiresias when last the city was visited by the 'Dog-faced witch' (the Sphinx)?

At this point, the Chorus intervenes, warning both men that intemperate words, discharged in the heat of anger, will do no good. Surely they should, instead, be seeking to meet the god's demand.

Teiresias tells Oedipus that it is not Creon, but Loxias (Apollo), whom he is pleased to serve. Oedipus may mock him for his blindness, but Oedipus is the one blind to his own 'damnation'. He prophesises that the eyes of **Oedipus, now 'clear-seeing', shall be 'darkened'**. Oedipus will be **'trodden down'** and the scorn of all will be upon him.

Oedipus heaps more ridicule on the seer. Then Teiresias utters the grimmest of prophecies. The man who once came to this town with his sight intact will leave as a blind beggar, stick in hand, to a land of exile. He will be known as 'brother' and 'father' to his own sons, **'son' and 'husband' to the woman who bore him**. He will be unmasked as a **'father-killer'** and **'father-supplanter'**. At this point, Teiresias goes.

Stasimon (choric ode) 1

The Chorus speaks of the hunted man, the 'doer of deeds unnamed', who will be unmasked. The son of Zeus (Apollo) is surely close behind him and such a man must soon be flushed from his lair, for 'deathless voices' cry out against him.

The Chorus admits that they can see no clear path ahead. Is it possible that there was a quarrel between the house of Labdacus (father of Laius) and the house of Polybus (the supposed father of Oedipus)? They confess that the whole matter confuses them. As to prophecy, they are unsure about relying on the words of Teiresias. They will 'impute no blame' until the matter is proved. Oedipus has to his credit that he 'faced the winged Enchantress' when all else had failed. They will think nothing but good of him until it is proved otherwise.

Commentary

Dramatic irony

The scene in which Oedipus demands to know who did the fatal deed, or who knows of him, is full of ghastly irony (as explained above). Worse still is his curse upon the culprit, for he is giving voice to the workings of divine punishment (not knowing that he will be the one punished). Then comes the culminating irony: if he or his are implicated, then **upon his head will lie 'all the curses' he has 'laid on others'**. A Greek audience would have practically groaned to hear these words. It is so painful to see a man harm himself. Here we are seeing Oedipus actually organise the process by which he will be destroyed.

When Teiresias appears, things move forward in a major way. So far, in the closed world of the play (ie what the characters themselves know, as opposed to what the audience knows), there have been no clear indications about who committed the crime. Now the truth is revealed. Teiresias pronounces judgement upon Oedipus – laying out for all his grim predictions of what is to come.

Oedipus' fatal flaw' revealed: hubris

The scene begins well enough, with Oedipus flattering the seer, saying 'all heavenly and earthly knowledge' lies within the old man's grasp. However, Teiresias – knowing the truth – refuses to answer Oedipus' questions. Instead of seeing a terrible warning in this, Oedipus sees it as impudence. It does not take long for his kind words to be retracted and replaced by wild abuse. It is more than a lapse, this rush to judgement. It is a fatal blindness to what is really happening. The seer is providing him with a massive hint – telling him to 'back off'. Oedipus, rash, headstrong, bullying, tries to force the truth out of the old man – and gets what he deserves (the information he asked for). Even when the Chorus advises caution, he blunders on, mocking the seer and becoming more, not less, intemperate. Our early doubts about Oedipus here crystallise rapidly. He is a man quick to take offence and quick to pass judgement. (His slaughter of Laius and his retinue upon the road now seems more plausible.) He is arrogant, preoccupied with his own dignity, inflexible in the face of dissent. Here is the *hubris* (pride) which is the classic *hamartia* (fatal flaw) of the tragic hero. Here is the engine of self-destruction which is at the heart of tragedy.

The terrible significance of the prophecy

By the end of the Episode, Teiresias has identified the 'sinner' (Oedipus) and actually given a clear prophecy of what is to come (the 'fall' of Oedipus which will involve blindness, a reduction to beggardom, and exile). Yet the king does not even understand that.

In reply to the harrowing words, 'This day brings you your birth (of knowledge); and brings you death', he replies smugly 'I am content'. The gap between what Oedipus understands and what *we* see is now so great that we experience that 'pity and fear' which Aristotle described. We feel the tragedy of this fatal misunderstanding, and know that things can only get worse.

Multiple ironies

Consider the many ironies at work here. There is irony in the distinction between those who can see and those who are blind. Teiresias is the blind man who 'sees' truly. Oedipus is the sighted man who cannot 'see' – a man 'blind' to his own faults (now becoming very obvious) and blind to the fate (now spelt out) that awaits him. There is irony in Oedipus' words to Creon that he has never laid eyes on the murdered man. That man is his own father, and we, along with the audience, know full well that not only did he meet him on the road described by Creon, he also killed him there!

Why we are told the story's ending: the all important moral lesson

In many ways the exposition of the play's central themes is now complete. Perhaps this does not satisfy us, a modern audience, used to more 'conventional' dramatic structures. We hope that the dénouement of a play (the untying of the puzzle) will occur towards the end, almost certainly as a surprise, giving the story that satisfying 'wrap up' that we love. Teiresias has ended any such hopes by already laying out clearly for us the conclusion to the play. Oedipus will leave Thebes at the end, sightless and homeless. His 'now clear eyes' will be 'darkened'. If all this seems dramatically rather unsatisfying, we must remember to set aside such modern pre-conceptions when approaching classical drama. If pleasure was to be found for the audience of these ancient plays it was in the unfolding of what *they already knew*. There were to be no nasty surprises for them, already well educated in the mythology which was Greek tragedy's primary source. Their satisfaction came from something deeper than a narrative 'tease' – it came from moral assurance, the knowledge that justice had been served. Being shown the 'end', for all its oddity to us, was part of the play's moral argument – it underlined the tragic man's fatal inability to see what he should do to avoid disaster. Here, in the most obvious way, Oedipus is given the ultimate warning (a prediction of his destruction), and still he cannot mend his ways!

The argument of the Chorus

If we turn to Chorus, we see that they still argue a great faith in the power of the gods. This murderer will not escape the wrath of Apollo. Dread consequences will follow if human blood has been shed. As remarked above, there is here something of a contrast between their simple, humble faith (in the gods) and the more arrogant, self-absorbed attitude of Oedipus, who seems to suggest that they would be much better off putting their faith in him. In a weighing up of gods (read for that if you like Nature, fate, the universe) and man, the Chorus are a timely reminder of who is likely to, and probably should, win. Divine justice, or individual will – the Chorus come down clearly on the side of the gods and morality.

Of a like kind to their simple piety is the Chorus' enthusiasm for moderation. They will not take up an extreme position, favouring one side or another. For the ancient Greeks, moderation (the 'Golden Rule', the middle way), was a virtue esteemed above all others. It alone prevented one from falling victim to the lusty passions which might otherwise rage unchecked. It was the guarantor of wisdom, the companion to quiet reflection.

The role of the Chorus: articulating a moral subtext

Some modern students will wonder why the Greeks kept the Chorus. Was it mere traditionalism and ritual? However, they had a purpose that went well beyond providing a poetic lull between scenes. They represented the voice of the common folk, the observers, not the fatal protagonists. Their eyes were clearer and their attitudes more traditional. They are a gentle reminder of old-fashioned virtues (modesty, caution, piety, moderation), to set against the fatal extremism of the tragic protagonist.

Episode (Act) 2

Scene 1 Creon and the Chorus

Creon's outrage

Creon appears, having heard the **'slanderous accusation'** which has been made against him by Oedipus. He will not accept any such **'grievous imputation'** against his good name. The Chorus assures Creon that the words were 'spoken in stress', and were 'ill-considered'. Creon however wonders whether the accusation – that Teiresias lied at *his* (Creon's) 'instigation' – was made with some deliberation. The Chorus hedges at this point.

Scene 2 Oedipus and Creon

Oedipus accuses Creon

Oedipus enters and launches into a tirade against Creon, calling him a proven 'plotter'. His motive? To steal the throne. Creon entreats Oedipus to hear him out, but Oedipus will have none of it. He claims that Creon is behind these 'intrigues' against his house, and Creon cannot expect to get off 'scot-free'.

Oedipus demands to know how long has it been since the death of Laius, how much effort was made at the time of his death to find out the name of his assassin, and whether old Teiresias was plying his trade back then? Did he accuse Oedipus in those days? Or are these new found accusations? Creon replies that every effort was made to uncover the killer of Laius at the time of his death, but in vain. Teiresias was a prophet then, as now, and held in similarly high esteem. Oedipus dismisses this, claiming that Teiresias would never have dared to name him the murderer of Laius, were it not for the prompting of Creon.

Creon's
defence

Creon however argues that he has no motive. He is the brother-in-law of Oedipus. His sister Jocasta is queen. Creon shares in equal part in this honour and glory. Why would he risk all these royal privileges for the sake of becoming sole king? Such ambition is foreign to him, a 'moderate man'. If Oedipus harbours doubts he need only visit the Pythian shrine to see if the first message he had brought was true. Further, if Oedipus thinks him guilty of any 'compact' with the soothsayer, then he is willing to accept the death penalty. Oedipus would do better than cast out an 'honest friend', life's 'dearest treasure'. Time alone will teach Oedipus the error of his ways.

The Chorus'
warning

The Chorus intercedes at this point to observe that the words of Creon are 'fitting for a prudent man'. One who is hasty to judge is seldom right.

Oedipus'
intransigence

Oedipus takes no notice. Creon now forces the issue, challenging Oedipus to banish him. However, Oedipus says he would rather see him dead.

Scene 3 Jocasta and Oedipus

Jocasta enters. She chastises the two men for their unseemly quarrel. These are 'private troubles', she asserts. However Creon is not easily mollified. At the insistence of Oedipus, **the terrible choices of 'death or banishment'** now hang over his head and no one will believe him innocent. While the Chorus joins in, entreating Oedipus to yield and not to 'cast away' a friend, Jocasta pleads with her husband to accept Creon's plea.

For his part Oedipus will not be swayed. Do they, he asks, realise the meaning of a pardon from him (it would be as good as

Oedipus'
concession

an admission of guilt on his part)? However, for the sake of the Chorus and the people of Thebes (who have more than enough troubles to deal with) he will spare Creon, if only he departs from his sight. Creon leaves in high dudgeon. Meanwhile the Chorus explains to Jocasta how the troubles began. Wild 'surmise' and 'baseless calumny' have led to this grievous falling out.

Jocasta persists in her inquiries. Oedipus tells her that Creon has accused him of the murder of Laius, but has done so hiding behind a 'rascally soothsayer' (Teiresias).

Jocasta's tale

Jocasta seems relieved at this news. Oedipus should put his mind at ease, she says. Soothsayers cannot always be believed. She knows of an oracle who once prophesied that Laius should die at the hands of his own child and hers. Laius *was* killed, but not by her son's hand. He was murdered by 'outland robbers' at a place where 'three roads meet'. As for the child who was supposedly destined to commit this murder, Laius cast it out when not yet three days old, abandoning it on a mountain side with 'rivetted ankles' to perish. Thus all the evidence suggests that Apollo did not contrive this ghastly outcome. The child could not have killed his own father. The father, Laius, was killed by others. Oedipus need have no fear on this score.

Oedipus'
reaction

Far from pacifying Oedipus, these words trouble him immensely. He now questions Jocasta much more closely about the event – the place, what Laius looked like, whether he was alone. Her replies only alarm him more. All the details came from a servant, the only survivor of the massacre, a man who begged to be relieved of his duties upon the arrival of Oedipus. He is now a shepherd in the country.

Oedipus' tale

Oedipus begs that this man be recalled and proceeds to tell Jocasta his sorry tale. He was raised in Corinth, and rose to be a man of some eminence. One day, a drunken man told him that he was not the son of Polybus (his supposed father). His own parents denied the story, but the 'smart' remained, and he sought reassurance from Pytho, the Delphic oracle.

There, instead, he heard a tale of 'horror and misery': how he would one day kill his own father, marry his own mother, and become parent to a 'misbegotten brood'. On hearing this prophecy, he fled Corinth, only to journey in the neighbourhood where Laius met his fate. He can well recall the place where the three roads meet, and how he met there a herald, followed by a horse-drawn carriage. A rude exchange followed in which the ill-treated Oedipus killed both the old man in the carriage and, as he thought, every man attending him.

Oedipus suspects the truth

If it now proves true that Laius died by his hand, then there can be no 'more wretched mortal' than he, Oedipus. The very hands that killed his own father have embraced the dead man's widow! **If true, then he is an 'utterly foul'** creature who deserves nothing less than **'banishment … from home'** and from his 'fatherland'. He would rather be dead than live with the stain of such infamy on his good name.

Advice of the Chorus

The Chorus agree that these are dreadful tidings, yet argue that they should still await word from the surviving witness before giving way to despair. Jocasta talked of 'robbers' in relation to the murderous deed. If there was more than one robber he is absolved of the deed. If it was a solitary wayfarer, however, the finger points directly to him. Jocasta assures him that the witness spoke of *robbers*, and repeats her assertion that the prophecy never came true. Still, to put their minds at ease, they should hear the shepherd's tale. To this Jocasta agrees.

Stasimon (choric ode) 2

In this ode, the Chorus prays that it may live **'with pure faith', keeping in 'word and deed' the Law,** which springs from the 'godhead' and is not of human making.

It is the sin of **pride** which the Chorus identifies as the chief vice which besets humankind. It is this sin which **'breeds the Tyrant'**, who soon finds himself tumbling from the pedestal into the pit. Zeal for civic duty is one thing. But those who act in a **'high-handed way', disdaining true 'righteousness and holy ornament'** will not escape **'doomed pride's punishment'**. If wickedness is to replace virtue, then truly there can be no sweet harmony here on earth.

The Chorus calls on Zeus to awaken. Apollo's name is now denied, there is 'no godliness in all mankind' and he must come to their aid.

Commentary The interchange between Creon and Oedipus is both dramatic and revealing. It begins with something like reasoned debate (note the efforts by Creon to rebut the accusations of Oedipus). However, as violent emotions break out (in both men), debate gives way to a verbal brawl (**'I know I am right ….. You are a knave'**). The exchange reveals much about the character of each man. Creon is quick to anger, assertive, jealous of his reputation. But in discounting the accusations of envy and sabotage, he gives away quite a lot about his personal characteristics: he enjoys the status and perquisites of office with none of the onerous duties attendant upon it. Perhaps there is a hint here of laziness – certainly of smugness.

Oedipus' pride revealed again

The portrait of Oedipus which emerges is even less flattering. What we already suspect about him – that he is a man of overweening pride – is borne out by the way he is prepared to execute his own brother-in-law (**'I would have you dead'**) without further ado. He seems like a man willing to exercise his authority in a quite tyrannical and intemperate manner. If we want to excuse his conduct, it can only be on the grounds that he is feeling the weight of recent accusations bearing down upon him. However, insofar as his actions argue arrogance, wrath and rashness – and they do – we are uncomfortably reminded of those cardinal sins, and their connection with catastrophe (the Aristotelian argument about tragedy).

The narrative is advanced as the truth emerges

In that regard, indeed, the dialogue between Oedipus and Jocasta moves the play closer and closer to its terrible *crisis*. Despite Jocasta's assurances (that prophets can't be believed, as her story of the dead child proves), in fact the very opposite becomes more and more obvious. We feel a sense of inevitable doom, like the hangman's noose, tightening around the necks of this impotent couple. Each effort by Jocasta to soothe Oedipus' fears only serves to heighten them. She reassures him that he need not fear the accusation of being the murderer of Laius! Her husband was killed at the place where the 'three roads meet'. Yet that is exactly where Oedipus remembers slaughtering an old man and all his party! By now, Oedipus has guessed the truth.

> Quote
>
> On me is the curse that none but I have laid...
> Is this my sin? Am I not utterly foul?...
> Can it be any but some monstrous god
> Of evil that has sent this doom upon me?

All that is lacking is confirmation. It is worth noting how his tone changes in the latter part of the Episode. We are reminded of the 'good' Oedipus we first saw. His horror, his now pathetically thin hope (that the seer will be proven wrong), are foremost in our sense of him. The bluster and 'macho' posturing with Creon is gone. Only the dread remains. At this point, as intended, our pity is reawakened. We begin to feel the tragedy, as he is feeling it.

The Chorus' argument

The second stasimon which closes off this episode is interesting. Once again, the Chorus reaffirm religious values, asking to live 'with pure faith', upholding in 'word and deed' the Law which is made by no human hand. This is conventional piety, certainly, but also a reminder that 'wickedness' is always a problem, and 'virtue' always to be preferred. We can strip away the machinery of the Olympian (Greek) deities referred to (Zeus etc) and still have a perfectly valid argument: morality is an eternal ideal.

Perhaps even more pertinent to the tragedy is what they say about pride:

> Quote
>
> Pride breeds the Tyrant…Pride tumbles to the pit…
> Who walks his own high-handed way, disdaining
> True righteousness and holy ornament…
> Shall he escape his doomed pride's punishment?

Hamartia

This could hardly be more explicit. Here is Aristotle's *hamartia* laid out with extraordinary directness. Pride goes before the fall. High-handedness will be punished. They do not refer specifically to Oedipus. They can't, and they don't need to. That is the connection *we* are meant to see. Jocasta and her dead husband, in their pride, thought they could outsmart the gods (in the matter of the curse). Oedipus, in his pride, thought the same, and then killed out of arrogance. The curse is coming true, and these two wretches are its focal point. For the original crime of scorning the oracle, and for an arrogant belief in their own rightness, this pair will pay a heavy price indeed.

Episode (Act) 3

Scene 1 Jocasta's plea to the gods

Jocasta carries a garlanded branch and incense in supplication to the gods. She tells the audience that her husband, the King, is **'overwrought' with 'fancies' and 'can no longer sanely judge'** the affairs of state. He listens to every word that 'feeds his

6666666
6666
66666666

apprehension'. Without him, the 'master-pilot', the ship of state is dangerously adrift.

Scene 2 The messenger's news

A messenger from Corinth enters, asking the Chorus the way to the house of Oedipus. The Chorus duly obliges, and he is greeted by Jocasta.

Ostensibly good news

The news he bears is that King Polybus of Corinth, the father of Oedipus, is dead. Jocasta reacts with an outpouring of relief. **What are we to make of 'divine prognostications' now,** she asks. They have been shown to be worthless. The man Oedipus feared killing for years has died of natural causes! At this point Oedipus enters and is also apprised of the good news. The death of Polybus did not come about as the result of 'foul play', rather the kind of illness which will end an old man's life.

Scene 3 Oedipus and Jocasta

Like Jocasta, Oedipus rejoices in the seeming defeat of prophecy. Oracles and 'prophesying birds' have been shown to be worthless. He had no role to play in the death of Polybus, and thus the 'letter of the oracle' is unfulfilled. He has nothing more to fear, except the prophecy about marrying his own mother, and Jocasta assures him that he has nothing to fear on that account. **It is 'chance' that rules our lives,** she assures him (not some kind of divine predestination).

Jocasta rejects the prophecy

The mind of Oedipus is not, however, completely at ease. The messenger is puzzled to hear of his fear of a woman. Oedipus tells him the tale of Apollo's prophecy and how fear of its fulfillment has long kept him from Corinth.

The messenger tells his tale

The messenger seeks to reassure him that he has nothing to fear from Merope, nor did he ever have anything to fear about contact with Polybus. They never were his blood parents. It was he, the messenger, who handed the young babe Oedipus over to Polybus and Merope many years ago. In those days the messenger was but a 'hireling shepherd' who rescued Oedipus from a mountaintop in Cithaeron. He was found there with his 'ankles .. rivetted' and to the subsequent infirmity he owes his name, Oedipus (swollen feet).

Oedipus is astounded at this news and asks who was responsible for leaving him there. The messenger says Oedipus would be better off asking the other shepherd to whose care he had been entrusted. The shepherd is none other than the one Oedipus has recently called for, the sole surviving witness to the massacre of Laius.

Jocasta understands the truth at last

By now **Jocasta is 'white with terror'**. She tells Oedipus that if he wants to live, he must cease his inquiries. Oedipus however insists that he must 'pursue this trail' to the end, until he has 'unravelled the mystery' of his birth. Even if the tale proves him to be of humble origin it should in no way impugn Jocasta and her royal connections. He calls for the shepherd to be brought before him. Jocasta is appalled. Before exiting the stage, she pleads with him one last time. If he will not abandon this quest **he is 'lost and damned'** for all time.

Oedipus remains ignorant – and blunders on

The Chorus confesses itself puzzled at this dramatic exit by Jocasta. It senses some 'vile catastrophe', about to be revealed. Oedipus, however, insists that the truth, no matter how vile, must come out. He is a 'child of Fortune', his sisters are the seasons, and all that he asks is that he should know who he is.

Stasimon (choric ode) 3

The Chorus argues that by tomorrow all will be revealed. They will know by then if their king is humbly born, or whether he is the offspring of some 'primeval sprite', perhaps the very child of Pan. A very short stasimon, it sings the praises of Mount Cithaeron as a kind of mother to the young Oedipus.

Commentary This episode begins with Jocasta's prayers to the gods. What a change is here! We recall that the scoffing at oracles and all their portents began with her rather than with Oedipus. Then she consoled herself with the thought that no man 'possesses the secret of divination'.

Underneath her somewhat desperate words of praise for 'Bright Shining Apollo' is a real sickness of heart. Has she has already divined the sequence of events which is about to unfold? Will the 'curse of this uncleanness' lead to revelations of past misdeeds too terrible to hear? Or is it her fear that the 'master-pilot' (Oedipus the king) is 'distraught', and the ship of state adrift? We are reminded of how fragile were the affairs of state in those days of autocratic kingship. So much depended on the guiding hand of the ruler. Once that hand trembled, all in his kingdom were imperilled.

The tragic irony of their false sense of security

With the arrival of the messenger from Corinth the final pieces of the puzzle are virtually complete. Oedipus' supposed father (Polybus) is dead. Oedipus consoles himself with the news. He is apparently 'off the hook'. He cannot have killed a dead man. By implication, both he and Jocasta were correct in their original judgements. No one should put their faith in oracles. Jocasta, in a sickening reversion to her 'godless' self-assurance, now joins with him in gloating over these revelations.

These few moments of rejoicing, enjoyed by both Oedipus and Jocasta, are deeply disturbing for audience and readers acquainted with the true story. It is timely to think about how the playwright here underlines the ignorance and vulnerability of humankind. Even great and powerful people (the king and queen) can be horrifyingly wrong. Such proud and jaunty reassurances (about their rightness and the 'oracles' – therefore gods' – wrongness) will ring hollow when the true state of affairs is revealed. We don't need the author to underline the moral here. It is loud and clear.

The philosophical subtext – man and gods

Beyond the drama, and the painful irony, something else is happening in this scene. A fascinating philosophical debate is being broached. When Jocasta rejects the messengers of the gods, declaring that it is chance (not the gods) which 'rules our lives', and that the future is 'unknown' to us, she is taking a position which is startling in its modernity. No existentialist philosopher of our times could have expressed it better. All we can do is to live our lives 'as best we may', living from 'day to day', in a universe lacking any divine plan. However, we must recall that she is speaking this way in a deeply religious and ancient culture. By expressing such atheistic notions she is flying in the face of religious piety. It may not strike us this way, but it certainly would have to the original audience. The play seems to suggest that we ignore the gods (and their prophecy) at our peril.

Dramatic irony

Having (falsely) put to rest his fears about his father, Oedipus now turns his attention to his mother. No Greek audience could have heard the words of Jocasta – telling him that all these thoughts of 'mother-marrying' are the stuff of dreams – without shuddering. For it was his mother, to whom he was married, speaking! No modern audience can watch (or read) the scene without sensing yet one more irony – of which even the playwright himself was unaware! For the entire edifice of modern

Textual resonance of the play

psychoanalysis was built on the interpretation of dreams, and it is precisely this play that gave Sigmund Freud his famous theory of the 'Oedipus Complex', in which every boy is said to harbour a desire to murder his own father and have sexual relations with his own mother! (Notes are provided under Themes.) Very few works of literature have quite the resonances of this one, for it taps the most profound issues of philosophy but also of psychology, including the most celebrated 'Complex' of all!

The descent into catastrophe

The situation, already bad – though the characters themselves are oblivious to the fact – now gets worse. Ironically, in trying to cheer Oedipus up, the Messenger unveils the next fatal piece of the puzzle. Oedipus can come back to Corinth any time he likes, for Merope never was his blood relation. Oedipus was abandoned as a child on Mount Cithaeron, and they were only his foster parents.

Notice Jocasta's reaction. Her determined optimism crumbles instantly. All of the pieces of the puzzle are now in place. She well recalls that it was she and her husband who left a child thus on Mount Cithaeron. If the tale of the messenger is true, then there can be no doubt that her husband is that same boy, now fully grown. Of course she does not say this. We deduce it. But her words:

> Quote
>
> Doomed man! O never live to learn the truth!...
> O lost and damned!

Oedipus' continuing proud insistence

are unambiguous. Poor Oedipus. All he sees is that she is squeamish about the possibility of him being 'slave-born'. Headstrong, assertive and cocky to the end, he pushes on to unravel 'the mystery of my birth'. Had he been more inclined to listen, less rash, would he not have taken Jocasta's stricken condition as some sort of clue? Oedipus, alas, as his whole fate makes clear, is not that kind of man.

The third stasimon is a very short one. Throughout Oedipus remains on the stage while the Chorus sings the praises of Mount Cithaeron. She was father, mother and nurse to Oedipus. Perhaps he was born of the gods, of 'mountain-haunting Pan'? Perhaps he is the very child of Apollo! Their words seem quite inappropriately cheerful to us as Jocasta is seized by despair and Oedipus obsessively seeks out his origins. However, for Sophocles, such ironically cheerful displays before the final tragic tableau were part of his dramatic armoury.

Episode (Act) 4

The truth

The shepherd's tale

The old shepherd enters. The messenger agrees that he is the very man who had once handed him the babe, Oedipus. The old man confirms that he was 'born and bred' into the service of Laius, and served as a shepherd on Mount Cithaeron. The messenger recounts how, in the past, they drove their separate flocks up on those mountains. But when the messenger insists that the old man handed him the baby all those years ago, the shepherd, horrified, denies any knowledge of these events. Only under threat of torture or death does he confess.

The sorry tale emerges. He did hand the baby over to the messenger. The child was from the house of Laius, not a slave, but the very child of the king himself. The baby was handed to him by its mother, with orders that it be destroyed. A 'wicked spell' had foretold that the child would one day kill his own father and she delivered the child to him for safe keeping. He had not the heart to murder the child, and gave it away to the messenger who, in turn, took it to another country where it was safe. If Oedipus is the grown man sprung from that baby, then his life is 'lost'.

Oedipus understands at last

Oedipus cannot contain his horror at these revelations. He has been unmasked as 'sinful' in the act of being conceived, sinful in his marriage, and sinful in the shedding of his father's blood. He leaves the stage.

Stasimon (choric ode) 4

This stasimon is a general lamentation by the Chorus. In tones of deepest disillusionment they bemoan the possibility of happiness. **All happiness is 'illusion', only to be followed by bitterest 'disillusion'**. If any man should have been happy, surely that man was Oedipus! He was the man who, with 'supreme sureness of aim' had chased every prize to be won, mastered every enemy, and won the esteem of every citizen of Thebes as their 'bastion against disaster'. This same man, folded into the breast of both wife and mother, has been found out in due course. Collectively they curse his presence, wishing they had never laid eyes on the offspring of Laius, **once their 'morning of light', now their 'night of endless darkness'**.

Commentary

The final dénouement

This quite brief Episode has a clear structural function: the 'dénouement' (or unravelling of the knot of mystery). Hints there have been aplenty about what really happened, but here the brutal facts are laid out once and for all. The dread hint in Jocasta's parting words (Episode 3) is fulfilled. Oedipus was indeed the child of Laius and Jocasta – the shepherd's evidence makes plain – and therefore it follows was the murderer of his own father and the lover of his own mother. His words at the end of the scene are minimal – but awful. Gone is the bluster and hope. Nothing is left but the horror.

We might well ask ourselves why Sophocles has placed his 'explanation' here. The play still has some little time to run. Why not have the dénouement at the very end, as in a modern mystery story? The answer is really that the mystery and the tragedy are not the same thing. Oedipus now knows the truth – and we might think that is the worst that can happen. But far worse is to come. His strange words '**O Light! May I never look on you again**' are one clue, as were Teiresias' in Episode 2 ('**Those now clear-seeing eyes shall then be darkened**'). And there is still the chilling echo of Jocasta's parting words ('**This is my last and only word to you forever**'). The truth is part of the tragedy. His and Jocasta's reactions to the truth, and the issue of 'punishment', remain.

Philosophical questions: the value of knowledge

If we turn to the philosophical implications of what has happened, we find ourselves in deep waters. The conventional wisdom of 'Know thyself' here opens up terrible dilemmas and has surely never seemed so bitterly ironic! Long considered to be the origin of true wisdom and right action, self-knowledge implies that only when one knows oneself one can then judge other things and other people. One will not be swollen with excess pride, nor inhibited by false modesty. One will have faced truths, pleasant and unpleasant, have learned to accept them, and have developed a proper sense of humility.

But truth (as an ideal) seems rather less glamorous in the light of what has befallen Oedipus. This was an obsessive seeker after truth, a man who would not let matters lie, as Jocasta advised. And he has been 'hoist on his own petard'. He has sought the truth – and it has destroyed him. Does this argue that one should let sleeping dogs lie? Probably not. Oedipus had little choice, given the pestilence and the (implied) inevitable working out of the gods' will. More likely it is a pointer to the underlying pessimism of the Greek world view so forcefully expressed in Stasimon 4: to know the truth is to know that we are fated to unhappiness.

The pessimism of the ancient Greeks

This is not the only challenge (philosophically) for a modern audience. Schooled in the Western tradition of free will and conscience, sin and atonement, we cannot help asking ourselves: can Oedipus really be said to be guilty for actions beyond his control and beyond his ken? He did not ask to be abandoned on Mount Cithaeron. When he mistakenly thought he was in peril of murdering Polybus and marrying Merope, he fled Corinth to avoid such a fate. The quarrel with Laius and the royal party reveal him to be a hot-tempered fellow, but he never knowingly slew his own father! The question of the guilt of Oedipus is later examined in the 'Themes' section of this book. For the moment we should consider these questions: Did his actions, either in the past or the 'present' of the play reveal any fatal flaws (*hamartia*) for which his fate might be considered a divine punishment? And is it possible that a cruel fate could befall a person despite their essential goodness? If the answer to either is yes, then the 'problem' of Oedipus' guilt is not quite the vexing one it first appears.

How guilty was Oedipus?

Significance of the choric ode

The fourth stasimon is laden with grief and lamentation. As was so often the case with a hero of Greek mythology, his fate is generalised to the fate of all of us. What has happened to Oedipus shows us that 'the generations of mortal man add up to nothing'. This provides a grim but not misleading insight into the nature of philosophical thinking in the ancient world. Like the biblical prophet in *Ecclesiastes,* they wonder whether all happiness is 'illusion'. How can any of us be happy, they reason, if this man, most blessed by the gods, is so stricken?

Most disheartening of all, they now seem to desert Oedipus. Having praised him as their once great leader, a 'bastion against disaster', they now disown him and wish they had never laid eyes on the 'offspring of Laius'. The fate of Oedipus in some way reaches out and threatens them all. These were the citizens of Thebes who turned to him in their hour of sorrow at the beginning of the play. His torment is not his alone, it threatens to reach out and taint them all.

Episode (Act) 5

Scene 1 The Attendant's report

A royal Attendant appears, telling the Chorus to weep for the news he brings.

Death of Jocasta

Queen Jocasta is dead, dead by her own hand. Barely had she left their sight than she entered her own chamber, and there went straight to her bridal-bed to lament the son born of her dead husband, the son by whom she conceived other children. Soon after Oedipus broke into the bridal chamber, demanding to see his wife, the 'soil' in which he was sown, and whence he reaped his own 'harvest'. There he saw his wife/mother swinging from a noose.

Self-mutilation of Oedipus

As he cradled her in his arms, he took from her dress the golden brooches with which it was pinned. At arm's length he then thrust them into his own eyes, piercing his eyeballs 'time and time again'. **Unable to bear 'his shame, his guilt' he blinded himself, until the blood run down his beard, a 'whole cascade descending/In drenching cataracts of scarlet rain'.**

Thus two have sinned, and now on two heads has fallen **'mingled punishment'**. Calamity, **'death, ruin, tears and shame'** are their legacy. As for Oedipus, he clamours for the doors to be opened, that all of Thebes may gaze upon the murderer and incestuous sinner. He wishes to fly the country, to rid his house of the curse he has laid upon it.

Scene 2 Blind Oedipus

The Chorus is horrified at the spectacle of Oedipus. They recoil from the **'foulest disfigurement'** which greets them and wonder what **'demon of destiny'** has borne him down. Oedipus himself is lost in a **'dark intolerable … night'**, filled with **'piercing pain'** that tortures body and soul.

The Chorus wonders how Oedipus has come to commit this terrible deed. What use can he have with eyes, he says, when all around him is ugliness? He begs to be led away, away from this land. He is a man who is 'lost', hated by the gods. No man is more damned than he. He curses the 'benefactor' who once loosed the child's ankles from the rivets which bound them. Death would have been a 'boon', had it come sooner. Surely, the Chorus suggest, it would have been better to die than 'to live in blindness'.

Oedipus'
self-loathing

Oedipus retorts that he could not meet his father 'beyond the grave' with his sight intact, nor his unhappy mother against whom he had committed such a **'heinous sin'**. How can he gaze upon his own children, knowing how they were conceived? How can he bear to remain in the city of Thebes when he, the king, has already declared the murderer of Laius to be an outcast? If it were within his power he would also destroy his own hearing, to block his ears to their cries of denunciation. If he could, he would imprison his body in **'total blankness'**, there to allow the mind to dwell beyond 'the reach of pain'. As they shrink from his grasping hands, he begs the Chorus to take him away.

In desperation and relief the Chorus notes the arrival of Creon. To him they will turn for advice on what must be done. He is now their 'sole protector'. Oedipus, however, can see no hope. He who has wronged Creon utterly cannot hope for clemency.

Scene 3 Creon's judgement

Oedipus' fate

Creon does not reproach Oedipus. Nonetheless, the 'unclean' must 'not remain in the eye of day'. Oedipus must be ushered indoors where none but his kinsmen should witness his suffering.

Oedipus is grateful for this show of respect. It is more than he could have asked for. He wishes to be cast out immediately, away from this land, **'out of the sight of man'**. Creon informs him that his wish will be granted, but he (Creon) awaits instructions from the 'god' (presumably Apollo). All Oedipus asks is that funeral rites be provided for Creon's sister, the unfortunate woman whose body lies within the house. For himself he begs to be allowed to go and **'live upon the mountain'**, the mountain on which he was abandoned as a child – Cithaeron. There, in accordance with his late parents' wishes, he will finally die. Yet even now he knows that he will not die like any ordinary mortal. He was not plucked from death all those years ago unless it was to be preserved for some even 'more awful destiny'.

For his own sons Oedipus harbours few fears. They will be able to fend for themselves. But his poor little daughters have never known a day without their father. He begs Creon to take care of them and to allow him to touch them once last time.

Scene 4 The children

Oedipus and
the children

The daughters of Oedipus, Ismene and Antigone, have already been led in. Creon has brought them, knowing how much Oedipus loves them. For this Oedipus tearfully thanks him. He begs the children to feel the hands of their 'brother'. It was that same 'brother' who 'darkened' the 'clear eyes' of their father. The father who did not know what he was doing when he begat them. He thinks of their 'sorrowful life' in the days to come, their limited chances for marriage with such a curse hanging over them and their offspring. They will live with this scandal all their lives and almost certainly face fruitless 'maidenhood'.

He implores Creon to adopt them. One day they will understand the full import of what has come to pass. Meanwhile they must pray that they live not 'more nor less than well'. If they do that, they will have lived better than their father.

The fate of the children

Creon intervenes at this point to tell Oedipus that he must now go indoors. Once more Oedipus begs to be sent away. Creon hesitates, but finally relents. He will allow Oedipus to leave, but not with the children. Oedipus is no longer in command. It is Creon's command that they now be separated from their father, and this command will be obeyed. The reign of Oedipus is over.

Exodos (final speech and exit of the Chorus)

Tragic summing up of the story

In closing, the Chorus asks the sons and daughters of Thebes to behold the pitiful sight which is Oedipus. The greatest of men, **he held 'the key to the deepest mysteries'**. He was the envy of all for his 'great prosperity'. They should contemplate what a **'tide of misfortune'** has washed over this man. From it they must draw the lesson that mortal man must look to the end of his life. **No-one can be called happy unless he dies happy and carries that happiness 'down to the grave in peace'**.

Commentary

In the closing stage of Euripides' famous play, *Medea,* the Chorus asks, 'What can be strange or terrible after this?' Those words could equally apply to the closing scenes of *Oedipus Rex*, especially the dreadful carnage described by the palace attendant. While the conventions of the day demanded that bloodthirsty acts occur *off stage*, their horror is, in some ways, heightened by the purely verbal descriptions of the attendant. It is left to our imagination to conjure up the pitiful sight of Queen Jocasta tearing out her hair and swinging from a noose. We see, all too vividly, Oedipus cradling her in his arms and then removing the brooches from her dress. The thought of him plunging those brooches into his own eyes beggars belief.

The power of tragedy

Tragedy is meant to provide 'fear and pity': fear at such horrors, yet pity that another human being could suffer so. It is the combination of the distance (like that of the Chorus), the revulsion, the moral repugnance – *and* the empathy, the feeling for the poor wretch, that makes great tragedy so profound in its effect upon an audience. In a world addicted to pleasure, to ethically empty 'entertainment', tragedy comes as a shock. It forces us to confront the pain of the world, the capacity of people to ruin their own lives, and while we know that they (here Oedipus) are not us (we are hopefully safe from such horrors), we feel for such

The use of tragedy

tragic individuals. And therein lies the use of tragedy. To see this final act of *Oedipus Rex* as just a 'gore fest' is to completely misread it. The hanging and the self-mutilation are not some 'shocko' excess, as in a modern horror flick, but a deeply felt symbolising of human pain. Here is suffering of an acute psychological kind, which then embodies itself in the physical (the taking of life, the blinding). It is the *suffering* which is the point of the play – not the noose or the blood.

Punishment and cleansing as a theme

Let us not miss either the moral symbolism of what is happening. The final scenes teem with cathartic images of washing and cleansing. The attendant assures us that not all the waters of the rivers Ister or Phasis can cleanse this dwelling of the evil acts performed therein. Oedipus is described as drenched with 'cataracts of scarlet rain'. The symbolism of purification is involved here, the washing away of sin. If we delve deeper, and consider what Freud said about the scene – suggesting that it is a symbolic castration (the eyeball as testis), we have yet another layer to the self-punishment. Also, there is the primary metaphor of sight. The man who was blind (metaphorically) has now blinded himself (literally) as an act of expiation (atonement). The self-mutilation is not just punishment, but also as an act of defiant self-will. This is the only action left over which he can exercise some control.

The tragedy through the generations

If all this were not enough for an audience already emotionally wrung out by these experiences, the children of Oedipus are now brought on stage! Their appearance, by the way, foreshadows the other great Sophoclean tragedies, *Oedipus at Colonus* and *Antigone*. The audiences of his day were well aware that *Oedipus Rex* is but one play in a trilogy known as 'the Theban plays'. They would also be well aware of the tragic story of Creon and Antigone yet to unfold. They also enable us to see Oedipus in a kindlier, more familial light. After all that has happened we see the final crushing and diminution of a good father, unable to keep his daughters by his side. The emotional impact is devastating.

The final irony, if ironies were not sufficiently abundant, is that the man Oedipus feared as usurper of the throne now emerges as his successor. In the absence of any other, it is Creon, brother of Jocasta, who must assume the throne. Not with foul trickery and misdeeds behind him, but with the gravity and demeanour of one already bearing the full weight of office. His manner is measured, there is no gloating over the spoils of office. It is a subdued Creon, fully aware of the awful gravity of the situation, but also a sternness that befits a just ruler. Oedipus may embrace his children one last time. They cannot accompany him. The humiliation and degradation of Oedipus the king is now complete.

Notes on Characters

Oedipus

What an extraordinary character is Oedipus! Even the formalism of Greek drama with its stilted conventions cannot conceal that fact. Across the pages of history he reaches out to us as a human being wrestling with a seemingly impossible conundrum. A man for whom the quest for truth will take him down any labyrinth, no matter the consequences for him and his loved ones. Indeed, before any finger of blame can be pointed at him, this essentially noble aspect of Oedipus should first be registered.

The noble qualities of Oedipus

The first glimpse we have of Oedipus the King is that of a man swift to action and gifted with insight. He appears as the ideal ruler of his age. His opening words to the citizens of Thebes – addressing them as children – establish his essentially paternalistic relationship to his subjects. He has saved them before. It is right that they come to him to be saved again. Even if his self-introduction smacks of *hubris*, he is clearly a natural leader. He has already sent Creon, his brother-in-law to the Delphic oracle for advice. He seems to embody many of the qualities which the author would have us esteem. We feel that we are being positioned to admire this man of action who seeks out the truth without fear or favour.

The ignoble qualities of Oedipus

Yet Sophocles is a crafty dramatist. No sooner have we admired these admirable qualities than his less noble aspects are revealed to us. This man of action can also be dangerously impulsive and intemperate. His reaction to the supposed scheming of Creon is vastly out of proportion to the threat posed to him. His call for a virtual death sentence to be passed on his brother-in-law, without a shred of viable proof, is not the action of a wise or modest ruler. The later story he tells of slaying the travellers on the road smacks of a hasty disposition and even fouler temper. We suspect that the reason he fled Corinth all those years ago is that he feared slaying Polybus during one of his regular outbursts!

This pattern of restless, ceaseless activity will be sustained throughout the play – together with the tension (in our mind) between Oedipus the good man and Oedipus the bully and sinner. He may be on a noble quest (the truth), but he is going about it in unfortunate ways. Barely has he finished condemning Teiresias, when his tirades of abuse against Creon begin. He hastily calls for witnesses to be summonsed, then dismisses them just as quickly. So swiftly does he jump from elation to the depths of despair that his judgement is impaired. Right to the bitter end he clings to shreds of hope where there are none. Once the fateful story can no longer be eluded he puts out his own eyes. He seems like a man trying to outrun the fates which are invariably going to catch him.

Oedipus and the theme of fatal pride

If we isolate the 'bad' side of Oedipus, we must acknowledge his pride. This fits of course completely with an Aristotelian reading of the text. For Greek tragedy was above all about *hamartia* (a tragic fault), and its brutal consequences. We see his arrogance in the very first speech:

> Quote

I, Oedipus, whose name is known afar.

and we even see it at the very end, when Creon has to rebuke him:

> Quote

Command no more. Obey. Your rule has ended.

He is a great man, with all the gifts but also the dangers that brings. It is not the only reading of the play, but it is an important reading, that Oedipus is exposed to us as a 'tyrant'. The original Greek title for the play was *Oedipus Tyrannos*. Only because of the Romans do we mostly know the play by its Roman title, *Oedipus Rex* (Oedipus the King). Look at Stasimon 2! It is pride which 'breeds the tyrant', according to the Chorus. He who walks in 'his own high-handed way' will not escape 'doomed pride's punishment'.

Oedipus commits other, more serious crimes (than pride). His twin crimes of patricide and incest are horrendous ones. But to the ancient Greeks, they proceeded from his cardinal sin, pride. Had he not tried to evade the divine prophecy, thinking himself above the gods, he would not have set off from Corinth. Had he not been an arrogant man, he would not have killed Laius *out of wounded pride*! Had he not fancied himself a hero, he would not have taken on the city of Thebes, and thereby ended up with its queen (his own mother)!

Oedipus the tragic hero (both good and bad)

Oedipus, in true tragic form, is *both good and bad*. His intentions, we can argue, were the best as he set out on his fatal investigation. He never meant to commit those terrible crimes. But what undid him was not *just* some divine curse. It was also in part his *hubris*. He accepts his punishment at the end not just because he is going through a ritual, but because he knows he has sinned – both in the precise nature of his crimes and in the underlying flaw of personality which led to them.

Jocasta

Jocasta's good qualities

Jocasta's first role appears to be that of peacemaker. She intervenes in the quarrel between Creon and Oedipus. She calms her husband in one of his most tempestuous outbursts. She pours oil on troubled waters.

Jocasta's weaknesses

However in her calm and reasonable manner may be found a clue to her own weakness. She does not want to face any truth which might be unpalatable. She does not want to believe that her life is in the hands of unknown forces, though her supplication to the gods is a contradictory gesture of conciliation. Repeatedly, she asserts that the gods are wrong, hence the prophecies, and all will be well. She does not see that the truth, so long concealed, must come out. Once she does perceive it, she is of no use to Oedipus whatever. Her soothing speeches are seeded with the cruellest irony. In seeking to dismiss what was once foretold about her own offspring, Jocasta has unwittingly told the tale of Oedipus and his own downfall. Her son/husband must pay the cruellest price of all for the efforts of she and her husband to outwit the fates when Oedipus was born.

Jocasta's challenge to the gods

Her fatal flaw would have had a deeper significance for the ancients. It is she even more than Oedipus who goes beyond what could be called healthy scepticism to fly directly into the face of the gods and their role in human destiny. When Jocasta pronounces that it is chance which 'rules our lives' and that 'the future is all unknown', she is throwing down the gauntlet to an idea of the sacred which had held sway for many centuries. She is the voice of the Greek Enlightenment, a period characterised by extreme wariness towards any received wisdom, a period in which many ancient beliefs were overthrown in favour of an increasingly humanistic and scientific view of world affairs. But she is wrong. Her rejection of the gods, her championing of human against divine power, is fatally disproved. In this perhaps we see the anxiety of Greek thinking at the time. Man seemed clever, dominant, noble. Yet would not the larger forces of the universe win out anyway? Could one afford to reject the gods after all? In effect, her suicide is the answer .

Jocasta
the victim

In many respects Jocasta is the real victim of the play. For that one action all those years ago – an action designed to thwart what must have seemed like a cruel and unjust fate – she must pay a terrible price. No wonder she is white with horror as the truth dawns upon her. Her beloved husband is that son banished to Mount Cithaeron as a babe. Their children are the progeny of an incestuous bed. Her wretched suicide is a prelude to the terrible fate which awaits Oedipus.

Creon

To a considerable extent, Creon is the pawn in the larger tragedy of Oedipus (and Jocasta), the observer of the catastrophe. However, of course, he is a character in his own right, and represents different qualities.

Creon as a
model of
cautious rule?

For a start he is cautious. We notice that when he returns from the temple of Apollo, he suggests to Oedipus that the news might best be aired indoors. It is Oedipus who insists that whatever business they have be conducted in the public arena. Creon's instincts, we might venture, are correct, though it could be argued that Oedipus speaks for a civic openness when he urges that the news be shared. Is this a choice between two models of government – one which seeks to consult with the governed – the other more autocratic but controlled?

Did Oedipus
have cause to
distrust Creon?

How dangerous is Creon? Oedipus is quick to suspect him, when the seer's words accuse. Certainly he is in many ways the 'power behind the throne'. He ruled Thebes in the absence of Laius. The throne was only handed to Oedipus as a gift for his great feat in ridding the town of the Sphinx. A gift can be taken back, and Oedipus may have good reason to fear his Machiavellian side.

Creon as a noble and 'moderate' man

However, the evidence of the text is that Creon is trustworthy. The worst he does is defend himself against the unjust accusations of Oedipus. When affairs unravel fatally, and he finds himself king again, he steps into the breech and smoothly establishes civic order. He takes no revenge on Oedipus (though he has reason to), and although there might seem something brutal about the way the fallen king is finally separated from his loved ones, in a sense it is only a reasonable position (how can a blind beggar look after two girls?). Creon is eager to reclaim the throne and establish his absolute authority, but he has not committed any error. And perhaps he could be seen as a 'moderate man', the sort of person who is far more reliable a king in the long run than an impetuous, error-prone, if heroic figure like Oedipus.

Teiresias

Despite the brevity of his appearance, Teiresias is one of the most arresting figures in this drama. There is something noble about this man and the kind of 'grace under pressure' which he displays.

To begin with, there is his reticence when brought into the presence of Oedipus. He does not want to tell all, knowing how devastating the truth will be. He is not cowed by Oedipus, nor quick to judgement. There is something resigned about the man. He is a prophet who has seen too much and too far, and who is burdened by the dreadful knowledge which he carries.

Teiresias as the instrument of tragedy

Although charged with the terrible knowledge of what is to be, Teiresias only tells it when he has no choice. He knows that the fates are fast gathering around the hapless Oedipus, and is helpless and sick at heart as the pre-destined tragedy plays itself out. What falls to him is the sickest and sorriest task of all. He must reveal all to the brusque, impatient man before him. The importunate king who will brook no delay, no dissembling. It is he, Teiresias, who must pronounce judgement upon this 'cursed polluter' of their land. Nor does Teiresias ever deviate from his purpose, once his course is set. He is not gulled by Oedipus' opening words, so full of empty flattery. He is no more impressed by the praise for his 'skill' in 'bird-lore', than he is by his later dismissal as a 'brainless, sightless, senseless old sot'.

The symbolism of Teiresias' blindness

Before leaving Teiresias, let us note the symbolism of his blindness. As has already been stated, Sophocles plays upon the irony of those who can see and those who cannot. Teiresias is physically blind. But that doesn't matter, for in the moral scheme of the play his eyes are fixed on the eternal verities – the will of the gods. It is Oedipus, not Teiresias, who lives 'in perpetual night' and who is about to be cast out into the darkness beyond human warmth and company. Oedipus is not a man who 'sees the light'. He dwells in the eternal 'night' of ignorance. Even our first physical image of Teiresias (an old man leaning on a walking stick) will be supplanted by the later image of helpless Oedipus, led away without even the comforting arms of his children.

So Teiresias is more than just the 'messenger of the gods' – though he is that too. He is a man who feels as well and whose pain (in contemplating what will happen) anticipates the full force of the final tragedy, when his words are fulfilled, just as his blindness anticipates the blindness of Oedipus. This '*doppelganger*' (double) effect, incidentally, is yet another of the play's remarkable parallels and symmetries.

Notes on Themes and Issues

Fate or Free Will?

> Chance rules our lives, and the future is all unknown.

In the opening scenes of this play we see a king at the height of his powers, assured in his judgements, at ease with the burdens of office. By the play's end we witness the pitiful sight of a man, bleeding from self-inflicted wounds, and leaning on his staff. He is utterly distraught, and we share his dejection and deep despair. How has it come to this?

Are they victims of a curse?

One answer is simply to say that these characters are the accidental victims of a horrid cosmic injustice. They never *intended* to sin. Yet a 'curse' set them on a path to destruction – the only question was how long it would take for the fatal outcome to unfold. No matter how much they twisted and turned, trying to evade the curse, it caught up with them anyway. Two ended up dead – the other blinded and in despair.

Were they responsible? Did they sin?

To what extent should we 'blame' Oedipus for the dreadful fate which eventually befalls him? For a modern person, steeped in scientific 'common sense', this aspect of the play seems to be unacceptable. How can we blame a man who did not *knowingly* commit any sin? As a baby he had no knowledge of the dreadful prophecy foretold about him. He could not be held responsible for his abandonment and eventual adoption. When he discovered the prophecy about his destiny, he took steps to avoid its coming true. He did not know the identity of the old man on the road, nor that of the woman he was to take as his bride. A rationalist would say that it makes no sense for him to be condemned for what ensues.

The Greek concept of gods

Was such a vision compatible with the thinking of the ancient Greeks? Well, yes and no. Their religion was not monotheistic (one God), but pantheistic (many gods). There was no concept of divine revelation, a chosen people, nor any notion of a Saviour or great prophet who would intervene in and guide human affairs. If anything, their theology derived from an earlier form of animism in which the gods (plural) dwelt in all living things, the seas, the mountains, the air we breathe. The gods also had a role to play in human affairs, although this was poorly understood. In addition, these gods were a capricious lot! They quarrelled, stole each other's wives, raped, plundered and pillaged. Their wayward nature was in effect a parallel to the precarious nature of human existence. Far from being a bulwark against disaster, a safe harbour in a stormy sea, the gods too could be blown by the winds of mischance. Thus the piety of which the characters in our play speak is really an act of supplication to the gods – a wish to be left well alone. The gods were there to be appeased, rather than loved or adored.

A deterministic interpretation of the play

Out of this rather grim and seemingly deterministic (ie predicated on human fate being controlled by larger outside forces) outlook a theatre was fashioned. Its most fundamental premise was this: that ultimately man is alone in a fairly unpredictable universe. He could make the best of his life, live well and piously, yet still a hideous fate might overcome him. This view of *Oedipus Rex* could be dubbed the '*Fate rules*' or '*Determinism*' view. The final words of the Chorus can be read as a bleak statement of this sort of fatalism.

A 'free will' or 'fatal flaw' interpretation

Yet it is possible to read the play quite differently. In this view, the characters have brought it all upon themselves. Jocasta and Laius sought to evade the inevitable fate decreed for their son all those years ago. They thought they could outrun a cruel destiny, one which would sweep them up in a tide of sickening destruction. They took evasive action, which only delayed the inevitable. In a quite misguided fashion, Oedipus, too, sought to escape his destiny. On hearing that he was to murder his father and marry his mother he fled Corinth, believing wrongly that the words applied to his adoptive parents.

This interpretation would see the actions of these characters as variations on the theme of *hubris*, an idea discussed elsewhere in these notes. All these people fall victim to an overweening pride, an arrogance that urges them to outrun and outwit the fates decreed for them. However, there are limitations to such an all-embracing notion, and these limitations must now be addressed.

This view could be called the '*Free will*' or '*Fatal flaw*' view. We can guess that Sophocles belonged to a tradition which still sought to honour the gods – not to see them as cruel and capricious. In such a view, they are above reproach, a sort of cosmic board of elders, wise and just. That leaves the cause of the tragedy firmly with the human beings – specifically the kind of wilful pride both Jocasta and Oedipus display throughout the play.

The text seems to argue pride and downfall

Effectively Sophocles is 'positioning' us to see that such pride will, indeed, get its comeuppance. It is best exemplified in the triumphant words of Jocasta that it is chance which 'rules our lives', and that 'future is all unknown'. She posits a kind of existentialist 'good faith' that we should simply lives 'as best we may, from day to day', with no thought for the fates or prophecies. And Oedipus, so great and confident in his own powers, is a living example of this. Yet all that can be brought undone by a stroke of misfortune, an act of arrogance or rash pride. In the case of Oedipus, it could even be argued that his doom awaited him from the moment of his birth. It only needed his eager inquiries to set off the whole tragic sequence of events.

Of course, different readers see different things in the text. There are no absolute answers to the question: fate or free will? In fact, Sophocles, a brilliant man and deeply thoughtful, would have acknowledged that in life generally, as in the particular workings of this story, arguments can be made for both positions. Yes we are controlled by forces larger than ourselves – and that includes the mysteries of heredity, which make us what we are. But yes, we also choose – and act – and either listen to advice and avoid trouble, or blunder wilfully on and come undone. It is best to keep an open mind on this central puzzle: to acknowledge that the play is in part of *'tragedy of pride'*, and also a *'tragedy of destiny'*. The precise balance, like the old debate over nature or nurture, may well be an eternal one.

Guilt and expiation

Quote

On no man else
But on me alone is the scourge of my punishment.

Whatever we may make of the foregoing debate about free will or determinism, there can be no doubting that Oedipus feels himself to be guilty. His words are clear at the end. He refers to himself as

Quote

A father that killed his father;
Despoiled his birth-bed; begetting where he was begot;

and talks of 'unspeakable acts' which he has committed.

Quote

Crimes have been committed. Punishment must now follow.

The ancient Greek view of guilt – the act is all

In fact, scholars tell us that the ancient Greeks were not particularly interested in motivation, let alone the 'extenuating circumstances' of what mental 'problems' caused people to commit crimes. They would have had no patience with the modern-day notion 'There is no guilty act without a guilty mind' (ie the principle of *criminal intent*). Excuses such as a person's unhappy childhood or abusive past being used to relieve that person of culpability (they committed a crime but couldn't help it argument) would have appeared absurd to them. To the ancients, the act was real, and to be accounted for. A thought was no better than a dream. Given an act of sin, an act of punishment was required before the cosmic balance was restored. For Oedipus to have said he was sorry would have been laughable. He must now pay, just as Jocasta knows she must. And so the suicide, and the self-mutilation.

Arguably, this ethical formula has endured, certainly in

*The modern
view of guilt –
intent is crucial*

Christianity, Islam, and indeed in the modern justice system. A crime is punished in an appropriate way. It not only acts as a 'deterrent', warning others against committing similar acts, but performs a sort of ethical credit/debit function (the debit of the crime is annulled by the credit of the punishment). Universally, people understand this formula. And it is no doubt properly the conclusion to the tragic story of Oedipus.

But is the punishment too much? Or is it in the wrong hands? Such questions are theoretical, of course. All we can perhaps say is that his crimes were just about the worst the Greeks could imagine – patricide and incest! And thus the brutality of the punishment. The fact that the punishments are both self-inflicted is itself significant, for it is an admission of guilt and the ultimate acceptance of the need for retribution. However grim the final scenes are from a modern, 'enlightened' point of view, we must bear in mind they serve a powerful ethical purpose – reaffirming the moral order (crime does not go unpunished, only virtue is rewarded) in what the ancient Greeks would have seen to be an essential way.

A tragedy of pride

Quote

Who walks his own high-handed way...
Shall he escape his doomed pride's punishment?

As already noted, Greek tragedy has been traditionally read as showing the working out of a tragic hero's 'fatal flaw', which is generally *hubris* (pride).

Now the play is problematic, even in this central matter, insofar as Oedipus could be said to be the accidental victim of unkind destiny (see 'Fate or Free Will? above). But there are still plenty of clues in the text to the idea of pride being his major problem.

*Was Oedipus
guilty of fatal
pride?*

Why did he run away from Corinth to avoid the prophecy? Yes it was to not be guilty of sin (a different thing to pride obviously). But it was also because he thought he could 'beat' the gods – a much more suspect motive. Why did he kill Laius at the crossroads? Because

> The leader [of the royal party] roughly ordered me
> out of the way;
> And his venerable master joined in with a surly
> command.

Oedipus is not one to be ordered. He is not one to be treated with disrespect. So far he is not different to most people. But what happens next?

> Quick as lightning, the staff in this right hand
> Did its work; he [Laius] tumbled headlong out of
> the carriage,
> And every man of them there I killed.

This argues a positively volcanic anger, and an absolute disregard for all others. They insulted him, the great Oedipus, and so they paid the ultimate price.

Why did he marry Jocasta? Yes it was logical, because she was a widow, and he a hero who had saved the city from the Sphinx. But for a young man to simply accept being king so quickly, and to take the queen as his automatic 'prize', again argues a remarkable degree of self-assurance.

His actions can be interpreted as inspired by pride

Then there are all the things he does within the 'present' of the play: tell the Chorus not to worry, he'll solve the mystery without further help (they in contrast want help from the gods); tell Teiresias (representative of the gods) that he is wrong and Oedipus is right; tell Creon that he's a rogue because the seer's words can't be right (Oedipus couldn't possibly be at fault); refuse to listen to anyone's advice, whether it be Teiresias or Creon or the Chorus; blunder on in his self-appointed mission to uncover the truth, no matter what it may be. And there is this extraordinary speech:

> I am the child of Fortune,
> The giver of good, and I shall not be shamed...
> Born thus, I ask to be no other man
> han what I am, and will know who I am.

This is almost preening self-assurance. The Greeks believed that such pride was an affront to the fates. To have a sense of how they would have shuddered to hear such lines, imagine a modern person saying

> I bear a charmed life. Nothing bad could ever happen to me!
> or
> I couldn't possibly fail. I'm good.

For all our modern rationalism, we still feel a horror at such arrogance, fearing that such a person is 'asking for it'. That's Oedipus exactly. He is 'asking for it'. And pride, that oldest of sins, which creates in him a fatal blindness, is what arguably brings him undone.

> Pride breeds the Tyrant...
> From castled height Pride tumbles to the pit.

The message, in Stasimon 2, could hardly be clearer.

The quest for truth

Quote

I must [go on with the inquiry]. I cannot leave the truth unknown.

Oedipus as the prototype of rational man

It is the work of rational man to expose that which has baffled others, to offer sound explanations for that which once seemed inexplicable. In these ways, and in the play under discussion, we can see Oedipus as a type of empiricist. He will not be distracted from his quest. He quickly gathers witnesses to help him uncover the truth. Despite his professed gratitude to Apollo for his assistance early in the play, he quickly takes the matter into his own hands and sets about unravelling the mystery.

Oedipus as the prototype of the 'detective'

Indeed, some critics have likened *Oedipus Rex* to a prototype of what was to become the classic detective story. It may be the earliest example we have of the lone 'detective' – in the classic tradition an incorruptible – setting out to solve the murder mystery. Pondering the mystery of Laius' killing, Oedipus begins to sift through the clues. However, he readily accepts the hearsay evidence that more than one gangster was involved, and proceeds on this basis. From this simple error ensues the long and unnecessarily complicated dénouement. The error allows Oedipus to blind himself to the seemingly obvious point that he alone *must* have been the killer on the road. It leads to his overlooking the vital clue that the lone witness to the crime, the servant, 'begged' leave to go away into the country and become a shepherd. Clearly the man immediately recognised the newly enthroned king and feared making accusation against him. This becomes a classic 'red herring' that keeps Oedipus off balance until the very end.

Is the playwright critiquing rationalism and modernity?

What is the intention of the playwright in establishing such a 'scientific' approach on the part of Oedipus? Is it to denigrate that approach, to show us its lack of insight. For the upshot of this search for truth is not glory, but the destruction of the seeker. The evil turns out not to lie in some dangerous 'other' who must be brought to justice and duly punished. The truth lies within, and thus the evil lies within. The very nature of 'civilised' man is thus satirised in this most conservative of plays. The quest for the rational, ordered solution leads straight to chaos. Jocasta herself can see it coming and flees Oedipus, 'white with terror'. Oedipus alone in his dogged pursuit to see the matter through to its end brings down upon himself destruction and infamy. From a quasi-divine position, assured of his power to judge, Oedipus is humbled, brought down by powers well beyond his reckoning.

So what is Sophocles saying about truth? Is Oedipus an inspiration for mankind – a hero who wants to find out the truth at whatever cost, and then accept responsibility for what he finds? *Various interpretations of the truth theme* Is he a noble example of the principle that painful knowledge is still better than blissful ignorance? Is he an illustration of the notion that truth is relative, that the 'innocent' Oedipus of the early scenes is the very same person as the guilty Oedipus of the end (which would argue the very modern idea that perception is all)? Is his story all about the absoluteness of truth, insofar as his whole quest is about stripping away illusions and revealing what really happened? Finding the truth is the central issue of the play. The text certainly affirms its importance, and effectively commends it, but there can be little doubt that a somewhat bleak view of life underlies the play. As the Chorus say in concluding

> Quote
>
> And none can be called happy until that day when he carries
> His happiness down to the grave in peace.

Taboos and the natural order

> Quote
>
> Nor need this mother-marrying frighten you;
> Many a man has dreamt as much.

The taboo of incest Throughout the ages and in many societies the taboo against incest has been very strong. Some biologists have even argued that it is to be found in other species of the higher primates. In other words, it is not simply a social construct, a product of a particular time or place, one which may be easily altered. It seems to be akin to a sacred family pact, one which is binding on virtually every human tribe or community. Like does not breed with like. Certainly it makes sense to the modern mind, for the risks of inbreeding and their genetic consequences have been shown time and again. Would it not then make sense that our childrearing practices, if not our genes, dictate that this most fundamental of taboos must never be broken.

The taboo of patricide

On a par with this taboo is the crime of patricide (father killing). The sin of fratricide is certainly the first 'crime' mentioned in the Bible, and we are left in doubt that Cain paid heavily for his sin, condemned to walk the earth forever branded with the 'mark of Cain'. Similarly the crime of patricide seems to strike at the 'natural order' of things. We recoil from the idea of son or daughter raising their hand in murderous rage against those who conceived and bore them. In addition, such a crime strikes at the very heart of family, the bulwark of the ancient world, the only safe harbour in a very dangerous world.

No one can read *Oedipus Rex* and miss its treatment of taboos. In traditional society, family is uppermost. Mother and father are sacred. The greatest taboos in any community are invariably incest (sexual relations with a family member) and the killing of a family member. Oedipus commits both crimes. It is impossible to overstate their significance. Together they strike a blow at the ties of blood and kin which, to the ancient Greeks, were the most sacred of all. If these pillars of the established order are demolished, who knows what mayhem will ensue.

The play as a reaffirmation of traditional values

What happens to him? When he realises what he has done, he doesn't hesitate. He punishes himself in the most frightful way, by putting out his own eyes. (Modern readers with an interest in psychology have argued that the eyes are analogous to the testicles, and that in a way his self-blinding is a coded reference to castration.) So the breaking of the taboos is followed by the punishment. Thus, the play reaffirms traditional values. Taboos are not to be violated, no matter how innocently. Violation leads to punishment.

To reduce the play to a sort of moral diagram is of course to ignore all its other qualities. But the 'argument' about taboos is important nonetheless. For the Greeks, tragedy was not an emotional orgy (like a bad soap opera), but a reverential treatment of significant themes. And one of these themes was invariably 'sin' and therefore what happens to sinners. Sin is punished. Whether it be pride (and Oedipus' pride is a notable cause of his misfortune, as argued previously) or the breaking of sacred taboos (as Oedipus breaks them, with both the sin of patricide and the sin of incest), the point of the play is that his sins are punished. To miss this aspect of the play is to fail to notice what would have been, to its original audience, just about its most important point.

A Freudian reading of Oedipus

The great Viennese psychoanalyst Sigmund Freud supposedly unearthed a childhood memory in one of his patients of being sexually aroused by seeing his mother naked. From this, Freud postulated what he came to see as a universal law of human nature. He called it 'the Oedipus complex', after the famous Greek myth.

The 'Oedipus complex'

According to Freud, every boy, during the so-called phallic period of his psychological development (3-6 years old), begins to see his mother in sexual terms, to be attracted to her, to want to 'have' her exclusively to himself. A corollary of this is that the father is perceived during this period as a rival, the other male who wants possession of the mother, and about whom the boy has fantasies not of possession but of elimination (if father dies or goes away, I will have mother to myself). However, there is a problem. The father is big and strong, and has power over both the boy and the mother. The boy realises that the father is dangerous. Indeed, in a fight over the mother, the father must win. This, Freud said, led to fears of castration – removal of the sexual threat posed by the boy.

How was the complex resolved? According to Freud, as the boy grew older he ceased to see the father as a rival, and *identified* with him instead, modelling his own emergent masculinity on the active, aggressive role model of the father. Thus the boy joined the society of men, and thereby earned the right to have his own woman, transferring his desire for the mother into desire for another woman. The complex was resolved, and the boy developed normally into adolescence and manhood.

Freud was convinced that his 'Oedipal' theory was central to human experience. He wrote to a friend:

Quote

> Here is one in whom these primeval wishes of childhood have been fulfilled, and we shrink back from him with the whole force of the repression by which those wishes have since that time [childhood] been held down within us....I have found in my own case too, falling in love with the mother and jealousy of the father, and I now regard it as a universal event of childhood...If that is so, we can understand the rivetting power of *Oedipus Rex*.

Because of Freud's huge influence during the early twentieth century, the 'complex' became famous, and although later questioned by just about every other branch of psychology, it continues to be a celebrated reference point for discussion of sexual taboos.

The power of the play to resonate with audiences

We must be very clear on this point. Freud did *not* argue that Oedipus was suffering from an 'Oedipus' complex! He understood perfectly that the 'sins' committed by the play's protagonist were unwitting ones. Nonetheless Freud argued that the play has held us spellbound for centuries, precisely *because* it resonates so strongly with us. It strikes a 'chord' in all audiences, argued Freud, because it is so close to the mark.

What the Critics Say

Analysing this classic play, Aristotle the famous Greek philosopher wrote:

'Fear and pity may be aroused by spectacular means; but they may also result from the inner structure of the piece, which is the better way, and indicates a superior poet. For the plot ought to be so constructed that, even without the aid of the eye, he who hears the tale told will thrill with horror and melt to pity at what takes place. This is the impression we should receive from hearing the story of the Oedipus'.

Aristotle The Poetics X1V

And speaking (for perhaps half the human race!) an influential modern thinker said:

'His destiny moves us only because it might have been ours – because the oracle laid the same curse before the birth as upon him. It is the fate of all of us, perhaps, to direct our first sexual impulses towards our mother and our first hatred and our first murderous wish against our father'.

Sigmund Freud The Interpretation of Dreams Volume 4 Penguin 1976

Laurence Kalmanson of the University of Chicago has written that:

'The spectacle of a hugely gifted yet greatly flawed human being struggling to do the right thing is still as theatrically powerful now as it was when Sophocles crafted his version of the timeless story. Whether the tragically flawed heroes of modern entertainment makes their stands in the arenas of politics, science fiction or opera, the mighty are still brought low by hubris, or pride and fate is still inescapable.'

Laurence Kalmanson The Oedipus Trilogy Research and Education Association 1996

Writing an Essay on the Text

1. Analyse the essay question closely

The quality of your essay will depend on how well you understand and then respond to the question set. It pays to look word-
by-word at the topic. Take this one:

> 'The **Chorus warns** that "**Pride** breeds the **Tyrant**",
> and **predict** "his doomed pride's **punishment**".
>
> **To what extent** is the **tragedy** of Oedipus the **result**
> of his **pride**?

Key elements of this topic are embedded in the words 'pride',
'punishment' and 'tragedy', as well as the additional ideas
signposted in 'tyrant' (an extension of the theme of pride) and
'result' (arguing a cause and effect relationship between his
behaviour and what happens to him).

You don't need to slavishly define each word. That is not the
point of the exercise. However it is important to have a very clear
idea of what these words mean, and test each carefully against
the text under examination. You might dispute Oedipus' 'pride',
arguing that he is just dedicated to his duty (of finding out who
killed Laius and being a good king), and claim that it is a 'tragedy'
of fate instead. Some effort should go into discussing the concept
of tragedy itself, and a better answer will undoubtedly refer to
Aristotle's formula.

2. Open up issues to be addressed in the topic

Nothing is prescribed. Every answer is different. But an essay
topic is a set of key ideas, and the more you have to say about as
many of these as possible, the richer your answer will be. One
way to do this is to ask a set of questions about the topic, as in:

Does the Chorus express the playwright's view?

Is Oedipus guilty of pride? How?

Is he a tyrant?
Can his downfall be seen as a punishment? For what?
Can his downfall be seen as an accident, or bad luck?
Is pride his only sin? Is it the reason for his downfall?
In what ways is the play a tragedy?

By merely trying to answer these questions, you will end up with lots to say about the topic, working gradually from the broad concepts down to the smallest details. Nothing else need be invented. Don't miss this vital stage.

3. Plan your answer from these notes

If all this activity has generated a page of scribbled note planning, that's a very good sign. But the creative brainstorming doesn't necessarily yield the best structure. Once it's finished, sit back and look at the points which have come up and ask:

Which issue should I start with?
What does that connect to naturally?
What would I conclude with?

In short, find the smoothest possible order. Number your points. Cross reference details. Find a neat way to package all these ideas.

When you have completed this stage, you are ready to write the response. You now have the mental map needed.

4. Build a series of paragraphs from your plan

Each paragraph must be about its own mini-topic. Each paragraph should have a topic sentence (explaining what it is discussing). This is normally the first sentence.

The introductory paragraph should open up and explain the topic, and give some indication of what you intend to say about it. The conclusion should sum up your argument (or opinion). Stick to your plan. Write from your notes. Check for spelling and other mistakes later. And good luck!

Sample Essay

'He that came seeing, blind shall he go … '

It is the blindness of Oedipus which leads to his destruction. Discuss.

<table>
<tr>
<td>

Introductory paragraph sets the topic in context – Oedipus' greatness, but also his 'blindness'

Topic terms picked up explicitly

</td>
<td>

At the opening of the play we are acutely aware of the power of Oedipus. He seems like a wise ruler, judicious and perceptive. Through the words of the priest we learn that this great ruler has shown wisdom in the past. He alone solved the riddle of the Sphinx and freed his citizens from her foul sorcery. Now, seated upon the throne of Thebes, he seems almost godlike in his power. He will first pursue the murderer of Laius, then, with equal vigour, trace his own ancestry. Yet this same king seems fatally flawed. He cannot 'see' that which is most apparent to his blind nemesis, Teiresias: that he is the source of the city's plague, that the illness which besets them lies within. By the play's end he will have awoken to his 'blindness', his awakening will be akin to a kind of spiritual self-realisation. He will come to know that it is he who is sinful, while those around him are blameless.

</td>
</tr>
<tr>
<td>

'Blindness' defined: arrogance/ pride

</td>
<td>

In what ways, then, can Oedipus be seen as 'blind'? To begin with, there is an arrogance about Oedipus which is not always attractive. From the outset he seems to place himself virtually on an equal footing with Apollo. He alone will solve this puzzle which has conquered lesser men. Did he not solve the riddle of the Sphinx once before? These are not the words and actions of a wise person. They speak to us of a man whose vision has become blurred. Perhaps he has allowed the pomp and panoply of his office to cloud his better judgement. Perhaps he is dazzled by his own visions of past success. Whatever the reason, we, like his Greek audience, are very aware of the fate which awaits those filled with stubborn pride.

</td>
</tr>
<tr>
<td>

'Blindness' in the headlong quest

</td>
<td>

In addition, there is a kind of blind zeal about his early quest. It is not undertaken in a spirit of humility, but with almost cocky insistence. He has it on the word of the Delphic oracle that the problem lies within the city of Thebes. He knows that the foul murderer is within the walls of his own fair city, yet his relentless

</td>
</tr>
</table>

quest would suggest that it were otherwise. The very nature of his pursuit suggests that the problem lies 'outside'. According to Oedipus, the problem is to be found in the evil scheming hearts of others such as Creon.

'Blindness' in his mistreatment of Teiresias

Then there is his questioning of Teiresias which seems quite out of keeping with the dignity of this most revered of men. We are positioned by Sophocles to see that Teiresias is no shallow huckster. His very reluctance to speak when interrogated by Oedipus is testimony to his undoubted integrity. We have seen him praised by the Chorus as one who 'lives the incarnate truth', and we have seen Oedipus concur with this judgement.

'Blindness' in going on to the bitter end

We must acknowledge also the reckless pursuit by Oedipus of the final chapter to the bizarre tale of his birth and upbringing. Even Jocasta can see the horror that lies ahead and begs him to desist. All that remains is for the old shepherd to tell the tale of his adoption and the final pieces will fall into place. Such is his zest for the truth, however, that Oedipus rushes headlong into the final pit of despair. He insists that he must 'pursue this trail to the end'. He would rather take his chances on being proven 'the child of Fortune/The giver of good', rather than accept the obvious fact that no good can come from this quest.

The symbolism of 'blindness'

Most telling of all there is the contrast between the literal blindness of Teiresias and the figurative blindness of Oedipus. Teiresias may be robbed of his sight, but he sees further and deeper than any other character in the play. Oedipus, the sighted man, can see the blind man in front of him but no further. He is a man blind to what fates await him, one whose intemperate language will come back to haunt him. It is a shocking fate which awaits the great hero. He will leave Thebes at the end of the play, a broken man leaning on a stick. The staff upon which the blind Teiresias rested will become, metaphorically, the staff upon which he will depend for the rest of his days. The man who was king of all he surveyed will not be able to see his hand in front of his face. The man who ruled his kingdom like a god will return to a state of childlike dependency on Mount Cithaeron. The mountain will, indeed, echo to his 'loud crying', as once it echoed to the wails of the infant abandoned on those desolate slopes.

Essay Questions

1. 'If Oedipus had not been so hot-headed and arrogant, the tragedy may not have happened.'

   Do you agree?

2. '*Oedipus Rex* is a mystery story with a tragic conclusion.'

   Discuss.

3. 'The Oedipus we see at the beginning of the play is a very different man to the Oedipus of the end.'

   How does he change, and why?

4. 'What infamy remains
   That is not spoken of Oedipus?'

   Just how guilty *is* Oedipus?

   Discuss.

5. The Chorus warn that 'Pride breeds the Tyrant', and predict his doomed pride's punishment.

   To what extent is the tragedy of Oedipus the result of his pride?

6. '*Oedipus Rex* argues that we must find out the truth, no matter how much it hurts.'

   Is this what you think the play argues?

Titles in this series so far

A Good Scent from a Strange Mountain
A Man for All Seasons
Angela's Ashes
An Imaginary Life
Antigone
Away
Blade Runner
Breaker Morant
Briar Rose
Brilliant Lies
Cabaret
Cat's Eye
Cloudstreet
Cosi
Diving for Pearls
Educating Rita
Elli
Emma & Clueless
Falling
Fly Away Peter
Follow Your Heart
Frontline
Gattaca
Girl with a Pearl Earring
Going Home
Great Expectations
Hamlet
Hard Times
Henry Lawson's Stories
Highways to a War
I for Isobel
In Between
In Country
In the Lake of the Woods
King Lear
Letters from the Inside
Lives of Girls and Women
Looking for Alibrandi
Macbeth
Maestro
Medea
Montana 1948
My Brother Jack
My Left Foot
My Name is Asher Lev
My Place
Night
Nineteen Eighty-Four
No Great Mischief

Of Love and Shadows
Oedipus Rex
One True Thing
Only the Heart
Othello
Paper Nautilus
Pride and Prejudice
Rabbit-Proof Fence
Raw
Remembering Babylon
Schindler's List
Scission
Shakespeare in Love
Sometimes Gladness
Strictly Ballroom
Stolen
Summer of the Seventeenth Doll
The Accidental Tourist
The Bell Jar
The Blooding
The Brush-Off
The Chant of Jimmy Blacksmith
The Collector
The Crucible
The Divine Wind
The Freedom of the City
The Great Gatsby
The Handmaid's Tale
The Inheritors
The Life and Crimes of Harry Lavender
The Longest Memory
The Lost Salt Gift of Blood
The Kitchen God's Wife
The Outsider
The Player
The Riders
The Shipping News
The Wife of Martin Guerre
Things Fall Apart
Tirra Lirra by the River
Travels with my Aunt
We All Fall Down
What's Eating Gilbert Grape
Wild Cat Falling
Witness
Women of the Sun
Wrack